Praise for SPIC-O-RAMA

1992 DRAMATISTS GUILD HULL-WARRINER AWARD
FOR BEST PLAY
1992 LUCILLE LORTEL AWARD FOR OUTSTANDING
ACHIEVEMENT OFF-BROADWAY
1992–93 DRAMA DESK AWARD NOMINATION FOR OUTSTANDING
SOLO PERFORMANCE IN A ONE-PERSON SHOW
1993 SPECIAL *THEATRE WORLD* AWARD FOR OUTSTANDING
NEW TALENT

"Phenomenal . . . Leguizamo has created the script that propels him into this alternately hilarious, scathing and heartrending satire."
—*Chicago Sun-Times*

"Compelling . . . Leguizamo has a flair for the ironic throwaway that leaves an echo of poignancy after the laugh."
—*New York Newsday*

"Mesmerizing . . . One of the hottest tickets in town . . . The laughs [Leguizamo] provokes seem filtered through ground glass, as if to make your soul bleed."
—*Variety*

"[Leguizamo] has enormous talent and reveals it with gusto."
—*New York Post*

"A self-reflective, comic and theatrical celebration of Latinohood . . . Leguizamo's writing indicates an insight into Latino family life which only an insider could offer and an eloquent writer could adequately express."
—*Metrópico*

"Acidly funny."
—*Daily News,* New York

"One of the season's sensations . . . wildly entertaining and memorable."
—*Chicago Tribune*

Praise for
MAMBO MOUTH

1991 OBIE AWARD FOR PERFORMANCE
1991 OUTER CRITICS CIRCLE AWARD FOR OUTSTANDING ACHIEVEMENT
1991 VANGUARDIA AWARD FOR WRITING AND PERFORMANCE

"Kaleidoscopic, hilarious and politically very incorrect."
—*Time*

"Fierce and funny. . . . Sentiment doesn't get within an arm's reach of the characterization, and yet . . . Leguizamo allows you glimpses of a heart still capable of tenderness."
—*The New York Times*

"Unabashedly funny."
—*New York* magazine

"This is savage stuff, but also very funny and exceptionally performed. . . . [Leguizamo's] characters [are] both human and true."
—*Daily News,* New York

"Bristles with the energy of secrets unleashed. . . . Satire that is supple as well as raw."
—*The Village Voice*

"Daring and original . . . poignant and startling."
—*Theater Week*

"Like Eric Bogosian, John Leguizamo is not only a vigorous and entertaining quick-change performer, but a genuine social critic as well."
—*The New York Observer*

"Razor-sharp, on-target and hipper-than-hip."
—*Show Business*

SPIC-O-RAMA

a dysfunctional comedy

by

john leguizamo

BANTAM BOOKS

NEW YORK • TORONTO • LONDON • SYDNEY • AUCKLAND

For information address: Bantam Books.

ISBN 0-553-37288-2

Published simultaneously in the United States and Canada

Bantam Books are published by Bantam Books, a division of Bantam Doubleday Dell Publishing Group, Inc. Its trademark, consisting of the words "Bantam Books" and the portrayal of a rooster, is Registered in U.S. Patent and Trademark Office and in other countries. Marca Registrada. Bantam Books, 1540 Broadway, New York, New York 10036.

PRINTED IN THE UNITED STATES OF AMERICA

Grateful acknowledgment is made for permission to reprint from the following:

"America" from *West Side Story* by Leonard Bernstein and Stephen Sondheim. Copyright © 1957 (renewed) by Leonerd Bernstein and Stephen Sondheim. Jalni Publications, Inc., U.S. and Canadian Publisher. G. Schirmer, Inc., worldwide print rights and publisher for the rest of the world. International Copyright Secured. All Rights Reserved. Reprinted by Permission.

"Brother Louie." Words and Music by E. Brown and T. Wilson. Copyright © 1973 by Finchley Music Corp. Rights Administered in the U.S. and Canada by All Nations Music. Rights for the World excluding the U.S. and Canada Administered by RAK Music Publishing Ltd. International Copyright Secured. All Rights Reserved.

"El Barrio Across 110th Street." Words and Music by Johnny Boy Maldonado and Eddie Arroyo. © Copyright 1991 by Love Mixx Music and MCA Music Publishing, A Division of MCA, Inc. All Rights Controlled and Administered by MCA Music Publishing, A Division of MCA, Inc., New York, NY 10019. Used by permission. All rights reserved.

"I Think I Love You" by Tony Romeo © 1970 Screen Gems-EMI Music Inc. All Rights Reserved. International Copyright Secured. Used by Permission.

Personal Power! Success Journal, vol. 3, cassette 1, days 5–7, by Anthony Robbins. Copyright © 1993 by Robbins Research Institute International, Inc., San Diego, CA 92122.

Photograph on page 21 used by permission of The Fresh Air Fund.

"Speak Softly Love" by Larry Kusik and Nino Rota. Copyright © 1972 by Famous Music Corporation.

(Note: Every effort has been made to locate the copyright owners of material reproduced in this book. Omissions brought to our attention will be corrected in subsequent editions.)

PRODUCTION NOTES

This text of **Spic-O-Rama** is based on the original one-man show performed by John Leguizamo. **Spic-O-Rama** was first produced, but not in its entirety, at the following theater spaces which are listed with their respective performance dates:

"La Misma Onda (The Same Wave)"—P.S. 122
PERFORMANCES—September 10 & October 8, 1991
CURATOR—Ela Troyano

Gas Station
PERFORMANCES—September 24 & October 3, 4, 16, 24, 1991
ARTISTIC DIRECTOR—Osvaldo Gomariz

Nuyorican Poets Café
PERFORMANCES—October 2, 17 & November 6, 1991
ARTISTIC DIRECTOR—Miguel Algarin

P.S. 122
PERFORMANCES—October 5, 12, 19, 26, 1991
EXECUTIVE DIRECTOR—Mark Russell

Dixon Place
PERFORMANCE—October 18, 1991
ARTISTIC DIRECTOR—Ellie Kovan

Gusto House
PERFORMANCE—November 2, 1991
ARTISTIC DIRECTOR—Andy Kollmorgen

Knitting Factory
PERFORMANCE—November 4, 1991

H.O.M.E. for Contemporary Theatre and Art
PERFORMANCES—November 8, 9, 15, 16, 1991
ARTISTIC DIRECTOR—Randy Rollison

"Moving Beyond the Madness: A Festival of New Voices" —New York Shakespeare Festival, Public Theater's Anspacher Theater
PERFORMANCE—December 1, 1991
CURATOR—George C. Wolfe
LIGHTING DESIGN—Dan Kotlowitz

On January 16, 1992, **Spic-O-Rama** opened at the Goodman Studio Theatre in Chicago and was performed in its entirety, which included slides and videos. It moved to the Briar Street Theatre, again in Chicago, on January 27 and played until March 15. On October 27, 1992, it opened at New York City's Westside Theatre/Upstairs, where it ran through January 24, 1993. **Spic-O-Rama** was performed for the last time, in order to be taped for posterity by HBO, at the American Place Theatre in New York City on February 8, 1993.

Goodman Studio Theatre, Chicago
PERFORMANCES—January 14–26, 1992
DIRECTOR—Peter Askin
LIGHTING DESIGN—Ken Bowen
ARTISTIC DIRECTION—Robert Falls
PRODUCTION DIRECTOR—Roche Schulfer
COSTUMES—Theresa Tetley
STAGE MANAGER—Deya S. Friedman
STAGE MANAGER, N.Y.—Michael Robin
The Latino Chicago Theater Company

Briar Street Theatre, Chicago
PERFORMANCES—January 27–March 15, 1992
GENERAL MANAGER—Phil Eickhoff
DIRECTOR—Peter Askin
LIGHTING DESIGN—Ken Bowen
STAGE MANAGER, February—Deya S. Friedman
STAGE MANAGER, March—Michael Robin
MUSIC SUPERVISOR—JellyBean Benitez
COSTUMES—Theresa Tetley
PRODUCTION DIRECTOR—Roche Schulfer
SET DESIGN—Linda Buchanan

Westside Theatre/Upstairs, New York

PERFORMANCES—October 9, 1992–January 24, 1993
DIRECTOR—Peter Askin
SCENIC DESIGN—Loy Arcenas
LIGHTING DESIGNER—Natasha Katz
SOUND DESIGNER—Dan Moses Schreier
VIDEO DESIGN—Dennis Diamond
MUSIC SUPERVISOR—JellyBean Benitez
COSTUME COORDINATOR—Santiago
VIDEO PRODUCTION—Chauncey Street Productions
ASSISTANT STAGE MANAGER—Theresa Tetley
PRODUCERS—Marshall B. Purdy
Michael S. Bregman
Westside Theatre

HBO taping at the American Place Theatre

REHEARSALS—February 5 & 6, 1993
TAPING—February 8, 1993
TV PREMIERE—May 15, 1993

ACKNOWLEDGMENTS

A real special SHOUT goes to Peter Askin and to the usual suspects for the usual crimes: Michael Bregman; David Lewis; Luz Leguizamo; Michael Robin; Theresa Tetley; Marshall Purdy; Philip Rinaldi; Lapacazo Sandoval; Sergio Leguizamo; Mark Russell of P.S. 122; Randy Rollison of H.O.M.E. for Contemporary Theatre and Art; the Goodman's Robert Falls, Roche Schulfer, and staff; the Gas Station's Osvaldo Gomariz; Ellie Kovan of Dixon Place; the Public's George C. Wolfe; Chauncey Street Productions; Albie Hecht; Magda Liolis; John Hazard; Johnny Ray; Terry Byrne, Rick Shrout, and the staff at Westside Theatre—you know who you are; David Klingman; Samantha Mathis; Linda Gross; Gina Velasquez Healy; Steven Vause; John Vicey; Caroline Strauss; Brigitte Potter; Chris Albrecht; Bob Levinson; Tom Hansen; Suzanne Gluck; and my loyal friend David Bar Katz.

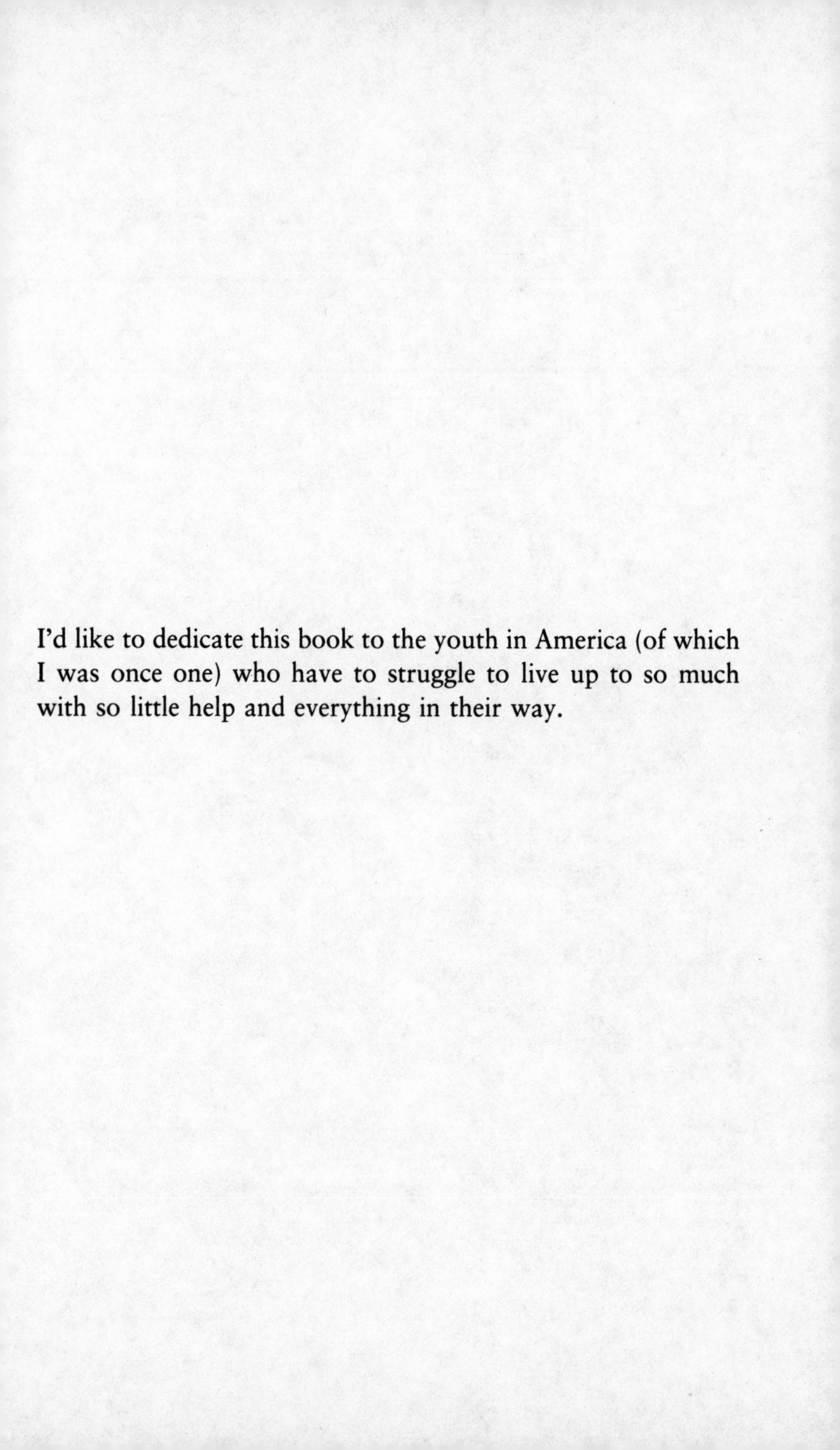

I'd like to dedicate this book to the youth in America (of which I was once one) who have to struggle to live up to so much with so little help and everything in their way.

CONTENTS

PREFACE BY MICHAEL S. BREGMAN

I first encountered John Leguizamo in 1990, while observing an acting class taught by Wynn Handman, director of the American Place Theatre in New York City. John would arrive in class with fragments of what would grow into *Mambo Mouth,* his first one-man show.

A few months later, after I had stopped sitting in on Wynn Handman's class, a friend of mine suggested I go see *Mambo Mouth* at Wynn's Sub-Plot Theatre, which seats about forty people. Now, getting me to go to the theater is about as easy as getting me to go to the public library on New Year's Eve, but I decided to go. In the months to follow I would return to see *Mambo Mouth* fifteen times. "Someone has finally done it," I thought to myself. "This guy has bridged the gap between Richard Pryor and Marlon Brando. He's a phenomenon!"

When John and his director, Peter Askin, asked me to produce *Spic-O-Rama* with them, I was delighted. I had never ventured into theater before, and never will again—unless John wants to do another show.

Since meeting, John and I have collaborated on six projects. He is not only my business associate, he is also my very dear friend.

MICHAEL S. BREGMAN

Producer Michael S. Bregman has made eight films with the Bregman Company. His producing credits include Betsy's Wedding, Sea of Love, Whispers in the Dark, The Real McCoy *with Kim Basinger and Terence Stamp,* Carlito's Way *with Al Pacino, Sean Penn, John Leguizamo, and Penelope Ann Miller, and the forthcoming* The Shadow *with Alec Baldwin. He is also executive producer of the HBO versions of John Leguizamo's award-winning plays* Mambo Mouth *and* Spic-O-Rama.

PREFACE BY ROBERT FALLS

For a one-man show, *Spic-O-Rama* was huge. It was a monster. It was, to quote Miggy, "spictacular." For three months in the dead of winter, it became the hottest ticket in Chicago. John's phenomenal talent attracted people of every color and age, from every neighborhood and income. And it provided the Goodman Theatre with a powerhouse introduction to Chicago's large and vital Latino community. Quite frankly, I've never seen anything like it. And *Spic-O-Rama* could have gone on forever.

I became friends with John during his *Mambo Mouth* days, and late in 1991 (while I was in New York) he took me out to a great salsa club. He said that he had a new one-man show he'd like to try out as soon as possible, and he wondered if the Goodman might be interested. In less than a month, John was performing *Spic-O-Rama* in our 135-seat Studio Theatre, in association with The Latino Chicago Theater.

John is miraculously talented, that's a given. But he's also remarkably savvy when it comes to marketing his work. John was interviewed by every Chicago publication and every radio and television station—both English- and Spanish-speaking—and if I read the phrase "born in Bogota, raised in Queens" one more time, I'll lose it. But all that publicity paid off. By the time *Spic-O-Rama* opened—to absolute rave reviews—the publicity had kicked in, word of mouth had taken hold, and the initial two-week run at the Goodman was sold-out.

With only two days of downtime, we moved *Spic-O-Rama* to the much larger Briar Street Theatre, where its popularity exploded. It was *the* show to see. It achieved cult status with a segment of Chicago theatergoers who returned time after time to see Miggy and his dysfunctional Gigante family, and it continued to draw a large Latino audience every night—at least forty percent by John's own estimate. *Spic-O-Rama* sold out its initial two-week run at the Briar Street in no time, was extended for another two weeks, and if John hadn't had other commitments, would probably still be running there today.

Spic-O-Rama was one of those extraordinary experiences that reaffirm your faith in your craft, your art. Its message was universal, and its heart was the blazing talent, boundless energy, and unfailing decency of its creator, John Leguizamo. I speak for the entire Goodman staff when I say that working with John (and with everyone he brought with him—Peter, Theresa, Robin, et al.) was sheer joy. For three months we all became hip-hop junkies. So, in the immortal words of the youngest Gigante, " 'M, to the 'I' to the 'G, G, Y' go Miggy!"

ROBERT FALLS

Robert Falls has been the artistic director of the Goodman Theatre since 1986, after serving in that capacity at Chicago's Wisdom Bridge Theatre from 1977 to 1985. His Goodman directing credits include The Iceman Cometh, Galileo, Landscape of the Body, Pal Joey, *the world premiere of* The Speed of Darkness, The Misanthrope, Book of the Night, *and most recently, the world premieres of* On the Open Road *and* Riverview: A Melodrama with Music. *Additional directing credits include productions for the Guthrie Theater, Chicago's Remains Theatre, the La Jolla Playhouse, and Broadway. Mr. Falls most recently directed* The Iceman Cometh *for the Abbey Theatre in Dublin, Ireland, and* On the Open Road *at the New York Shakespeare Festival.*

INTRODUCTION

I'm sitting here with John Leguizamo in a funky psychedelic Mexican eatery, El Poco Loco, translation: "The Little Crazy." That's just what it's been like these couple of hours—with the vibrant and festive colors on every wall and artifact, the loud fat *beat kicking out of the speakers, and the sumptuous repast before us, I feel as if I'm inside some giant's fecund mind. And the little giant, John, is dressed in his finest hip-hop-bad-boy garb, spewing hyperkinetically between mouthfuls of Mexican nouvelle cuisine for the nouveau riche.*

So here we are. I'll try to make this short and painful. Now, how did you start writing *Spic-O-Rama,* your second one-person thang? What was your first impulse?

It was March and I was six months into performing *Mambo Mouth* off-Broadway at the American Place Theatre and I needed some form of distraction. Some kind of new challenge. I kept changing the show *(Mambo)* but it wasn't enough for me. Until one day I saw a guy on the street in Desert Storm fatigues just hanging on the street corner with his boom box. It was *Waiting for Godot* Latinofied. Then I let him live in my mind, trying to figure out what he did for a living, what he would sound like. Then I remembered all my friends who went into the service and a whole new character came out—Krazy Willie. I started improvising and putting on his military wardrobe. He came to life. Then his story started to tell itself and from his story the other characters emerged.

Why another one-man show? Why not a full play? Didn't you have enough the first time?

What are you, a critic? Where do you get off not thinking it's a full-length play? It's a Latin *Long Day's Journey into Night*, but comic.

Yes, I appreciate that literary allusion, but try not to digress. Look, what I mean is, how is it a play as opposed to a series of loosely strung monologues?

I wanted to do something very different from *Mambo Mouth.* I still wanted the one-man-solo-monologue format, because it was a form I loved and admired. I feel it's the oldest form of storytelling. The most organic. It's the first man—Cretaceous or Jurassic—sitting around the fire chewing on a brontosaurus leg and retelling the day's events and acting them out. And I'm sure he was a smartass who made fun of everyone and got some handouts for being amusing or maybe they stoned him to death.

Peter (director and confidant) Askin also wanted to challenge me and take my writing to the next level, a more interconnected story instead of the random vignettes of *Mambo Mouth*. The story as a whole has unity and momentum moving toward an event: the wedding.

Yes, a plot! Thank God for a unifying theme or a little structure to sink your crowns on. Now, tell me, what other elements make *Spic-O-Rama* different from *Mambo Mouth*?

As I changed costumes and prepared for each new scene in *Mambo Mouth*, the audience saw the silhouette of someone dancing behind a screen. In *Spic-O-Rama* we replaced the silhouette with videos that keep the forward motion accelerating. The videos bridged the plot and also aided in camouflaging the costume changes which, with Theresa Tetley (*Mambo Mouth* silhouette bar none), we had down to between one and a half minutes (on the slow side) and forty-five seconds (our quickest). That's if everything went right, which it often didn't. Many a time, I came out with an open zipper or without Gladyz's wig or forgetting to tuck my nether regions into the spandex.

The videos provided a break from the one-man monotony and added a new voice and flavor. Seeing the people the characters in the show referred to deepened the whole experience. For example: Vanna Blanca, Javier's dominatrix girlfriend, explains to little Miggy what she does for a living: "I'm an escort. I escort people. It's like your mother. She gives you candy to go to the supermarket with her and . . . you . . . escort her to the market. And she'll give you candy or something for going. That's what I do."

And on men: "They need to be spanked on a regular basis. Unless they like it, of course."

Let's talk about your personal life.

Let's not.

Well, what I mean is how much of *Spic-O-Rama* came from your personal life? [John sits very stoically, making origami machine guns with his napkins. I'm sensitive. I pick up the subtle clues and move on.]

Okay, you knew this one was coming: Why the title? Was it for the controversy? Inquiring minds want to know.

What do you mean? What's so controversial about Rama, the ancient Egyptian god?

Don't try to skirt the issue, you little avoidance demon. I'm talking about the *S* word—spic. Why spic?

Plain good old-fashioned unadulterated controversy. I like the shocking and the raw. It's something that thrills me. It was daring and a bit offputting, and that's exactly why I liked it. Hence, *Spic-O-Rama.*

That's a nice pat answer, but really, what's the story behind the title?

Thank you for putting me in my place, Digression Police. Yes, the title's vicious because it represents overcoming the evils of life. The play is all told from a little boy's perspective and the little boy was me in a lot of ways.

Let me tell you, being called a spic at the age of nine was a total shock. We lived in a part of Queens that was just turning Hispanic and a lot of the remaining families were white trash. (See! Hispanics are like the cleaning bacteria at the bottom of the food chain. We move into neighborhoods that are dying and change them into something more lively and festive. We're like mushrooms [fungi]—beneficial to the cycle of renewal.)

So anyway, I was very friendly with the white-trash families (I had no choice—they were the only kids on the block). And whenever there was an argument back then, the swearing would turn to, "You spics, get out of my block! You're ruining the neighborhood." (Yeah, like we kept them from renovating. We held their hands back from painting their stoops and we hid their pens so they couldn't fill out job applications. Give me a break!) But that word would turn up time and time again and it affects your formative years—creates toxic shame. It pulls you right out of the moment and you say to yourself, "Damn! I didn't know I was a spic. How come my parents never told me? Yeah, I look different. But different is good, isn't it?"

The title also took something heinous and made it benign. Rendered a weapon harmless. Detonated a bomb. I'm from the Lenny Bruce and Richard Pryor school of thinking: If you use a word often enough, it loses it meaning and value. Richard Pryor used the word *nigger* in most of the titles of his works to reappropriate its negative effect. He took control of it.

The title was screaming for attention in a medium where we are not represented. Latinos are at least ten percent of the population of the United States—that's 26 million Latinos—but nowhere present in the media. So I figured I'd use a title that screamed, "Hey, someone's ignoring us. Why are we being ignored? Is there a subliminal curse on us? Are we carrying some stigma?" So naturally, *Spic-O-Rama* seemed important.

However, the title did give me trouble down the line. Without having seen the show, some Chicago news stations would not have anything to do with the play and Canada refused to air the HBO version solely based on the title. They wouldn't even look at it. And some Latino intelligentsia were like, "There he goes again, our prodigal son, denigrating us. We had such hope for him." If they missed the boat once, they'll miss it twice. If they didn't get *Mambo Mouth*, they won't get *Spic-O-Rama*.

Why a dysfunctional family? How did you arrive at this motley crew?

I picked a family—well, actually, the family in the play adopted me. Some of the most important theater works, masterpieces, have been about families, and almost all are semi-demi-autobiographical. They reveal the most and touch me the most. *Long Day's Journey into Night* and *Death of a Salesman* are my top two favorites. So I set out to create a comic tragic family that is closer to the way I perceive the world. Sort of funny and painful at the same time.

The family is where it all begins. It's what forms and drives us for the rest of our lives. *Oedipus, Hamlet*—you name the classic hero. Look at *Ordinary People*. We all have some wretched inner child who's angry or resentful or traumatized, and that is what drives us for the rest of our lives. No one is exempt.

What is your "process?" Do you test your material out? I mean, well, the question is more about development of the entire play from the germ of an idea, so to speak. Come on, give it up.

I always write my work down, go over a few drafts, and then my mad experiment begins. It always begins in a living room with tons of coffee and some appetizers to keep the audience of family and close friends awake and eager through these marathon all-night events. I read these twenty-page character monologues, giving them only a few intermissions to recaffeinate. Then the comments begin. I usually can't help but antagonize anyone with a negative comment. But I have to protect myself, don't I? I'm right, aren't I? I start arguing back and defending my work, but they're used to it. Well, at least I am.

Then I go furiously to work. Get notes from Peter and cut and restructure.

There are a lot of writers who find it difficult to kill their darlings: precious bits, lines and moments that they have spent years refining and can't find it in their hearts to cut. Is it difficult for you to edit your material?

No. My idea of cutting is to enlarge the margins and reduce the font. So the appearance of cutting is achieved and my little progeny will not be eviscerated. But Pierre (that's French for Peter) catches on and I have to reduce the script, usually by half. A process that feels like someone is cutting off an appendage.

When do you know you're ready? When to stop cutting? Does an editing fairy come in the night and take away your red pen?

Well, it never stops changing. That's the beauty of theater to me. It keeps evolving. I can improve it every night. Acting, writing, timing, lighting—everything.

But you digress. At this stage of my "process" I usually invite more friends for more coffee and more crudités. I'm still just reading from the script at this point because I don't want the focus to be on my acting but on the words and the story. And when I take away the script, my acting distracts from just what is written down. It's harder on the audience, but hey, what are friends for?

Then I'm ready to take it to the downtown clubs. I take my props and three or four of the characters at first and start to build from there. Don't wanna shoot my wad all at once. Usually my brother, Sergio, or Theresa Tetley or Michael Robin (stage manager for both *Mambo Mouth* and *Spic-O-Rama*) help me schlep across town with projector and costumes en suite.

Where are these enclaves of fermenting creativity?

First destination is downtown in the lesser-known and smaller venues (less audience, less criticism). I'm still vulnerable and must keep nurturing my work, even though I have quite a callus on my soul from doing improv and sketch comedy. The places I go to (thank God I'm in New York, the mecca of performance art spaces) are Dixon Place, the Gas Station, P.S. 122, Nuyorican Poets Café, and H.O.M.E. for Contemporary Theatre and Art.

And then I'm ready for a lot more rewrites and restructuring. Peter and I set appointments, break them, and rework the whole sucker. He helps and guides me. I stubbornly stick to my offspring and he plays along, knowing in the back of his head he'll get his way eventually. It's a perfect synergy. Peter and I are a perfectly complementary team. He's great with structure and my strength is dialogue and character.

You took the play to the Goodman Theatre in Chicago, where you performed it for the first time in its entirety. How did you get it there and how had it changed from the downtown clubs?

Well, it's a romantic story. I was performing a version of it at the H.O.M.E. and my caring, trusting, loving agent, David Lewis, invited Robert Falls (artistic director of the Goodman) to come and witness one of my readings. It was love at first sight. But like any relationship, demands and expectations get set up. And Bob (I can call him that) felt the story needed some tweaking. So Pedro (that's Spanish for Peter) and I mind-melded and restructured. The plot changed drastically, from being Raffi's wedding to Krazy Willie's wedding, which then made Krazy the main character and Raffi the other brother.

The videos we talked about earlier were finally added. We shot them with some old colleagues, Chauncey Street Productions, who had done a bang-up job with a special for the Comedy Channel called *The Talent Pool*. I used a lot of the actors from a comedy workshop I started and some kids from public schools. Picked the best of the bunch and they proved to be a wonderful addition. You just give them the material and let them paraphrase and improvise around it and you get gems—for example: In the video following Miggy's monologue, Eurasia says on the subject of family, "You can have a lot of fathers, but you have only one mother."

Some of the other videos were just interviews and yet others were elaborately set up, like the wedding, which was intercut with actual footage from a Bronx wedding.

How did it keep changing?

Lines kept improving. The whole fight between Miggy, the white kid, and Ivan was first a checkers fight and after the first month became a spitting contest. More jokes came to mind. "See, you don't have to go to a third world country to adopt me. I'm right here" was added shortly before opening night. My acting kept loosening up: Raffi became more flamboyant, Gladyz more vivacious, the father more bitter.

All except one piece improved. The one exception was a monologue, which I dedicated to my brother, about a physically challenged man. It came easily and effortlessly at first, especially in Chicago because I had just finished the three months of readings and was right on schedule in the "process." But on the reopening in New York and for about two months into the off-Broadway performance I struggled. I couldn't connect with the content until the last few weeks of the run. Then, out of exhaustion, I just gave in to the piece and let it take me wherever and it became something quite wonderful on its own.

What was the reaction from the public in Chicago?

We did the play for two weeks at the Goodman's smaller space which had about 135 seats. The two weeks were sold out before we opened with a waiting list of 600 people and phones ringing off the hook. This was all due to the *Mambo Mouth* airing on HBO and the Goodman's tapping, for the first time, into the huge Hispanic population of Chicago which was mostly Mexican and Puerto Rican with a smattering of Colombians and Cubans.

Do you have a system? A regime? I mean, how do you prepare for such an arduously physical task as a play?

I started running daily and working out like a fiend. I needed the aerobic endurance for this 105-minute show that could grow even longer, depending on the laughs. (Our longest show in Chicago ran 119 minutes, almost two hours.) And I had an ulterior motive—I wanted to look good in Gladyz's tights and midriff.

We then moved to the four-hundred-seat Briar Street Theatre. By this time, the reviews were coming out and they were exceptional. The consensus was in: Chicago would be our second home. The audiences were highly responsive—white, Hispanic, and black. The *Tribune* wrote a piece on the show talking about the multiethnic audience, teenagers on dates, the upper echelons of theatergoers in furs—it was like an ad for Benetton.

I got many dinner invites, offers to live with families, and the usual "What are you doing tonight?" (wink wink nudge nudge). I also got material gifts like jackets and what-not. (See! Celebrity does have its positive side.) But Nancy Reagan got in trouble for that, so I make sure I pay tax on those suckers.

Some people came with pots of homemade food—*arroz con gandules* (rice with pigeon peas), Puerto Rican soul food, *pudin*, etc. I was invited to try the many Colombian restaurants' ample menus. I always brought Theresa Tetley and Michael Robin. We had done *Mambo Mouth* together and we were doing *Spic-O-Rama* together and enjoying the success. If you don't have close friends to steal some of the credit, who can you enjoy your success with?

The mayor and governor declared March 15, 1992, to be John Leguizamo Day. That one day was like out of *The Wizard of Oz.* A proclamation was given unto me and I instantly felt I had . . . *(SINGS)* a brain, a heart . . . the nerve.

How did a hardened, inner-city New Yorker like yourself fare out in the mild-mannered Midwest?

I was suspicious of everyone's goodness and kindness (an old New York tendency). I kept thinking they're too nice—they must be up to something!

Why did you wait five months between the Chicago and New York productions?

I went to shoot *Super Mario Brothers* and returned five months later. I had to work hard to get back into the physical and emotional life of the play, because for some reason I didn't want to go to that bitter, angry place within myself. But I got it toward the last weeks before we closed.

What was it like bringing it back to New York?

I expected the worst from the reviewers in New York.

Why? They loved *Mambo Mouth*.

Everyone knows that after you've had one success they come at you much harder and expect more from you and try to crush you the second time. (I'm not paranoid!) I learned early on from other actors not to let reviews affect me, but you can't help but get affected. So I prepared for the worst and hoped for the best.

I saw your show in Chicago, and in New York I noticed that you changed the ending. Why did you do that? Are you an obsessive-compulsive perfectionist?

I was having a Dostoevskian episode trying to figure out the ending of the last piece of the play and it simply wouldn't come. It just lay there and sucked. We tried everything. Shortening it. Lengthening it. Saying it quicker. But it kept sucking.

Petrovich (Russian for Peter) was never happy with the ending of the play either. He felt it didn't quite close the story and leave the audience with a bang. We were toiling away constantly trying to improve it. Then he thought of ending it with something I had written for Miggy but could never find a place for, about his disgruntledness toward God, and boom—it fit and the show had an ending.

I heard you were trying to get the show at the Public. What happened?

We had tentative dates set for the Public. We were trying to do a Goodman and N.Y.S.F. collaboration. George C. Wolfe wanted the show and Joanne Akalaitis didn't. The talks went on and then I got *Super Mario Brothers* (which paid an incredible lot and eventually provided the money that produced *Spic-O-Rama*), so I went with it.

I worked on *Mario* from May to August. When I got back, the Public was no longer available. I had a few offers to take *Spic-O-Rama* to Broadway, but doing that meant giving the film rights away and doing eight performances a week for what I was sure would have been a minimum of six months with a condition to extend. And that kind of a lucky break was a bit of a problem. My instrument (if I may be so artsy) couldn't take it. During *Mambo Mouth* I went to several voice therapists. Changed my diet. No fried food or spicy food. No smoking. No caffeine. No drinking. No grunting during sex. The life of the ascetic was mine. To repeat this again gets tougher as you get older.

Even though I was miked, the physical demands of *Spic-O-Rama* always left me completely drained and hoarse. My methody self would start preparing at three p.m. for an eight p.m. show, so my voice would be raspy and my throat burned after every performance. The cumulative effect would make my voice get raspier and raspier as time went on. To do only four months and maybe six performances a week—all I could stand physically—was not a profitable enticement to producers, especially since Peter and I wanted the tickets to be as affordable as possible so that lower-income folk could make it.

It ended up that I became one of the producers along with the Westside Theatre and Michael S. Bregman (who went above and beyond the call of duty). I was scared, but I put the money I had just painfully earned on *Super Mario Brothers* into my own work because I believed in it. To be honest, though, the chances of getting my money back looked grim.

The show opened. We sold out all the previews to audiences which, surprisingly, were made up of eighty percent Latinos. Then the reviews came out and business doubled and we sold out the whole run. We nearly doubled our investment. Life is sweet.

What was the audience response?

Again what happened in Chicago. Offers from fans. I got Playbills with lipstick kisses and telephone numbers. Letters about the best sex I would ever get. Tempting. More material rewards, gifts: Some fans gave me cups engraved with *Spic-O-Rama*, towels with my name monogrammed, etc.

Did you ever get tired or bored doing it night after night for four months?

No, I kept finding new laughs. Better ways of saying certain things. I would ad-lib new jokes during performances. Peter also kept coming up with new and better ways of saying lines that made the show tighter and funnier. And he kept me fine-tuned like a lead guitar. The show got a little soft around the third month of the New York run. Like a comfortable pair of shoes.

Previews, by far, were the most exciting. But every now and then I had a great performance. Sometimes, it's just one character that really shines. But it's always up for grabs. Even though I prepare, things happen to me. Each audience has its own personality which affects me. If I had a bad day and was angry, it would be an angrier show. If something tragic happened that day, my performance would reflect that. That's what makes theater the most incredible kind of performance art. It's the most honest. On film you do take after take until you finally feel the right emotion or they can cut away from you if you just don't get it and infer it another way. But onstage the audience knows if you're there or if you're faking it.

And the things that go wrong make it a thrilling challenge. Gladyz was a real hazard—boobs kept falling down, her wig tangled on a nail on the set; I burned myself on the cigarettes, choked on the food. Once Gladyz pushed the carriage too hard by accident, overturning it, killing the baby, and spilling out all the props, which almost rolled off the stage. Krazy Willie's shirt got caught on the fence and for all my pulling, I couldn't free myself. Can you believe it—right in the middle of my most passionate lines! So I began to act like I was having a flashback, "All right, I'll give my serial number. Let go. I don't have any secrets," then ad-libbed, "I hate when that happens."

When I was there I saw Madonna. Who else attended?

I'm not name-dropping, I'm downright bragging. My idol, De Niro, came on the last performance. Came down to my dressing room. And in his most De Niroish way, which is very economical, congratulated me. (Another dream come true. See, visualizing works!) Martin Short, Brian Di Palma (couldn't get Coppola in, much to my chagrin), Mike Nichols who wrote me a very funny letter, Jodie Foster, Nathan Lane, the king of one-man shows, Eric Bogosian. See, this spic has pull, baby.

How did you prepare for the HBO taping?

We had to cut the script to fit the 55-minute requirement without losing the JPMs (jokes per minute). We lost Javier and the closing we had struggled so hard to get right. Had to include the camera angles into the performance—when I would look into the camera, when not to), that sort of thing.

How was the filming different from a regular performance stage?

The smaller audience, the smaller laughs. I had a fever and a cold. I'd been away from the material for about two weeks and had to get in the groove very quickly. We had four cameras rolling and the camera operators talked often and loudly, which is tough when you're used to just hearing yourself talk. Distractions of film changes, commands from the booth. Lights not working, the cameras going down during the show, etc.

It must be hard to be both writer and actor?

I don't know how Orson Welles and Woody Allen do it. They direct, write, and star in their own productions. It's tough switching hats. As the writer, it's one mind-set, and as an actor I have to reapproach the material totally fresh. Acting someone else's material is a million times less formidable.

What do you feel is the basic difference between TV, live theater, and film?

Theater is the actor's medium, film the director's and TV the producer's. Onstage it's you, by yourself. No one is going to save you by yelling "Cut!" or letting you do ten takes till you get it right. You're either in the moment or you're not. Which is really ideal, since you learn to respect yourself and leave yourself alone. Live performance is still the most organic of all the media. Because it's not done with machines or editing, it's got all the imperfections, all the mistakes, and all the magic of real talent.

El Fin

GLOSSARY OF FOREIGN TERMS

amigos y socios: friends and colleagues
asqueroso: disgusting slime
Ay, fo!: Euuu, yuck, p.u., it stinks, nasty
babas: dribble, spit
bendito: poor thing, blessèd
Bien nice y chévere: Real nice and groovy, kool
blanca: white (feminine)
bobo: jerk (masculine)
boricua: Puerto Rican. Derived from the Indian name for the island
bruja: witch (feminine)
cabeza: head (both literal and sexual meanings)
cabróncito: little motherfucker (masculine)
chaito: good-bye
chichichita: my little poopsie, my little bubeleh
cobarde: coward

condenado: weasel (masculine)
coño: damn, shit, fuck, piss, etc.
culo: butt, asshole
desgraciada: wretch (but stronger, with more disgust; feminine)
Dios mío!: My God!
Epa! Epa!: Groove it! Groove it!
Et tu: (Latin) And you (from *Julius Caesar:* "Et tu, Brute?")
Et voilà, mon frères!! Je suis ici: (Imperfect French) And look, my brothers!! Here I am
felicitaciónes: congratulations
gigante: giant
gordita: chubbikins (feminine)
guevón: big stupid bonehead
Hola: Hello
Imaginate!: Imagine that!
inútil: useless
jodona: kvetcher, annoying person (feminine)
la majadera: the rube (feminine)
las feitas: the ugly ones (feminine)
las morenitas: the dark-skinned ones (feminine)
las negritas: the black ones (feminine)
loca: crazy (feminine)
malparido: abomination
maricón: a pejorative for one who indulges in same-sex love
matrimonio: matrimony
Me cago en tu madre: I shit on your mother
Menealo!: Move it!
Metale semilla a la maraca pa que suene: Put the seeds in the maraca so it will go
Me tiene: He has me
mija: my daughter, my darling
mijo: my son, my darling
mira: look
Mira el mutant: Look at the mutant

mondongo: tripe (a Spanish delicacy non-Latinos find quite heinous—litmus test for true Latinoness)
mujeriando: wenching
muy: very, extremely
nada: nothing
nena(s): girlfriend(s)
niña: girl
No invente papito: Don't play me
No joda: Don't be annoying. Give me a break
No joda zángano, lo cojo y lo vuelvo mierda. Le hago que le salgan plátanos por el culo: Don't bother me, rascal, I'll catch you and beat the shit out of you. I'll make plantains come out of your butt
Oye, cómo va?: Hey, how's it going?
papá: endearment to loved ones (masculine)
papi: endearment used by parents; e.g.: little pops (masculine)
pendeja: dummy (feminine)
pendejo: dummy (masculine)
Pero, ojo: But, careful
por favor: please
porqué: because
Porqué tú me haz jodido y no puedo más. Y no es mi culpa: Because you have fucked me and I can't take any more. And it's not my fault
porquería: trash
Pues claro: But of course
puta: whore
Puta(s) sucia(s): nasty dirty whore(s)
Que Dios me haga más vieja antes de mi tiempo: May God make me older before my time
Qué embustera: What a deceiver
Qué linda: How pretty
Qué mentirosa: What a liar (feminine)
Qué precioso: How handsome

Qué rico!: How tasty!
Qué te pasa, nenita?: What'sa matter with you, baby?
Qué's eso?: What's that?
Regarde: (French) Observe
Sabrosito!: Delicious!
Sana que sana, culito de rana (si no sana hoy, sanara mañana): Heal, heal, little toad-butt; if you don't heal today, you will tomorrow
santera: a witch doctor or shaman (feminine)
Santería: a religious practice in Latin American countries taken from African voodoo, native South American folklore, and European Catholicism (it works, for a small fee)
Sí, es sad, verdad. El primero, tú sabes: Yes, it's sad, right. The first one, you know how it is
Tan bonita la niña. Tan preciosa. Ay tenía que ser mia: So pretty the little girl. So precious, oh she had to be mine
Tú eres un maricón, malparido y guevón: You are a faggot, abomination, and have some nerve
Tú lo mereces: You deserve it
Tú sabes: You know
una enema grandisima!: a huge enema!
Un sinvergüenza: A wise guy
verdad?: right?
yo debo: I oughtta
zángano: rascal (masculine)

homey, homes, homeslice, G, B: forms of "homeboy," used by Chicanos in jail in the fifties to mean "from my hometown," appropriated by African-Americans in the eighties and by everyone else in the nineties

I'mma school her: I'm going to teach her

in the house: when someone is ruling the scene, someone makes an appearance or is guesting

kick it back: answer back

Lookaher: Look at her

musta: must have

sex up: to have sex with

shout out: make a toast to, dedication

skankless: without filthiness

skeeze: to sleaze, sleep around

smokin': hot

suckerbutt: smells like a butt, looks like a butt, is a butt

This is the shit!: This is what's happening!

Waz up?: What's up?

weasel: cheat, act sneaky or snaky, get one's way underhandedly, be very Machiavellian (e.g.: Nixon weaseled in the White House)

wichoo: with you

word: form of agreement (e.g.: A: "She was fly!" B: "Word!"); that's the truth; really

youse: all of you

SPIC-O-RAMA

a dysfunctional comedy

GLOSSARY OF SLANG TERMS

axed: asked
be the flavor: be the star of the situation
buggin': getting mad, going crazy (e.g.: "He's buggin' " as in "He must be crazy")
burnouts: homeys, fellas, posse of worn-out potheads and whatnot; losers
coochie: buttocks, gluteus maximus, tush
dissed: disrespected
dogging: do something bad like cheat on people, disregard them
fesses: confesses
fugly: contraction for fucking ugly
gonna: going to
gotta: got to
ho: whore

"There is no greatness without a passion to be great, whether it's the aspiration of an athlete or an artist, a scientist, a parent or a businessman."

—Anthony Robbins's Personal Power! Success Journal Volume 3, Cassette 1, Days 5–7

Prologue:

MIGGY

(Audience and stage are completely dark. Rap music sounds in the background and we hear the voices of children at play in a school yard. Miggy leaps onto the stage and appears to fly through the air as he dances hard, lit by a strobe light which catches him in midair when he jumps. After the adrenaline of the audience is pumped by this seemingly impossible stunt, the lights come up and we see nine-year-old

Miggy wearing a long blue stocking cap, thick translucent blue glasses, teeth with overbite, Day-Glo orange oversized jeans, yellow-and-blue flannel shirt buttoned to the top, and high-top sneakers. Miggy is standing center stage with a row of industrial-yellow-colored dryers on his left, a chain-link fence with a beat-up old car parked behind him at center stage, and a bed with a white-framed window to its side on his right.)

MIGGY: *(To his teacher, at rear of audience:)* What?? What?!! But Mister Gabrielli, I've had my report ready—you just never axed me. *(Pulls down screen for slides. Under breath:)* Suckerbutt. *(To Mr. Gabrielli:)* I didn't say nothing.

(To class/audience:) "Monsters, Freaks, and Weirdos," by Miguel Gigante. My science fair project is loosely based on my family. And any similarities are just purely on purpose.

(Aside to a nearby classmate:) I can too do it on my family. I can do my project on anything I want, welfare face.

(To class:) My *(Looks at scribbling on his hand.)* hypothecus will prove, class of 501, that no child should have to put up with the evil inhumanation that I live with every day. Especially a nine-year-old genius with the potential of myself. *(Pats himself on the back. Aside to same classmate:)* You're just jealous 'cause you live in the projects. *(Sings:)* Your father is in jail, your brother's out on bail, and your mother is a ho!

(To class:) Last year I axed Santa Claus for a normal regular family, but I guess I must be punished for something I don't even know what I did. So I got all these mutants for family. And at exactly five o'clock, carloads of the most nastiest freakazoids are gonna come to my house for my brother's wedding and so I'mma run away and the next time you see me I'm gonna be on the back of a carton of chocolate milk. *(Aside:)* Shut up! I'm getting to

it. Oh, my God, I'm sorry, Mister Gabrielli! I didn't know it was you. How was I supposed to know it was you? I didn't smell your breath. *(Digs in his butt as he turns on slide projector and approaches screen.)* Okay . . . What?

(To class:) This is me, of course. With my handsome pre-Columbian features. See, you don't have to go to a third world country to adopt me, I'm right here!

This is my brother, Krazy Willie. We call him crazy 'cause he is. I share my room with him and this is his fake homemade Soloflex. *(Runs to stage right, which is decorated as a boy's bedroom. Jumps up on the single bed, then jumps to reach chin-up bar hanging from the ceiling. Does one pull-up and counts out loud:)* Eight, nine, ten. *(Then drops to bed, leaps off bed, and runs back to center stage.)*

He went to Desert Storm and it's the most important thing he's done in his life. But my father still calls him a loser. He's getting married tonight and I'm not gonna have anybody to protect me no more. Word. 'Cause he lets me hang out with him and watch him get high and sex up the females. *(Maniacal giggles.)*

This is his female, Yvonne. He calls women females so he don't get confused. And this proud eleventh grader can be seen at Show World nightly.

These are his burnouts. That's Chewey and that's Boulevard. Waz up? Waz up?

This is his sex mobile. Someone stole the motor so it don't work, so they just hang in there and pretends to go places.

This is my other brother, Raffi—brains not included. I have to share my room with him, too. And I don't dislike him. I just hate him intensely. 'Cause if he's not talkin' about himself, he's talkin' to himself. And he's weird, 'cause he thinks he's white. *(To random audience member:)* Oh, yeah, even whiter than you, mister! *(To class:)* Word. One day, he locked himself in our room for hours and hours. And when he finally came out, he was screaming, "Look, look! A miracle, a miracle! The most sacred lady of Flushing has appeared before me, transforming me into an albino white person." And he has blond hair and blue eyes. Na-ah! Na-ah! Not even. 'Cause I searched our room and found that miracle—holy water by Saint Clorox.

This is my other brother, Javier. He didn't let me take a picture of him so all I got was a picture of his finger. And he don't live with us 'cause he's like those freaks and monsters they keep in dungeons and broom closets and they scream and yell and live off of bugs—that's him. He's my brother, but it's not my fault 'cause you don't pick 'em, you just get 'em, and sometimes they come out irregular like Javier.

Oh, guess who else is coming to the wedding. My bugged-out aunt Ofelia. She became a santera—that's a black magic healer—'cause she couldn't get no dates! Word, she's got magical powers. I'm serious. Look into her eyes. Oooh, you're getting sleepy. Oooh, you're getting sleepy. *(Slide goes in and out of focus.)* You are under my power. Take off your clothes, everybody! *(To Mr. Gabrielli:)* I was just playing, Mister Gabrielli. *(Under breath:)* Suckerbutt.

Eeeuuu! That's my uncle, Brother Gonzales. He makes me call him Uncle Brother. He's a really mean evil guy who loves money. So he charges for confession. Look, watch this. *(Addresses slide:)* Oh, Uncle Brother? Oh, Uncle Brother? I'm here for confession. What is this? *(Pulls dollar bill from pocket.)* It looks like a dollar. Look at him come after it. Come on, you greedy pig, come and get it.

See, I learned how to work that religion thing this summer.

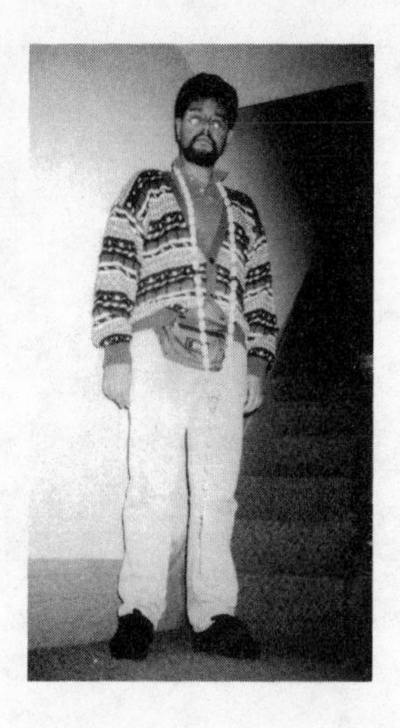

This is my cousin, Efraim. I can't show you him 'cause he's an illegal alien, all right? *(Quickly passes to next slide.)*

This is my mother, Gladyz. *(To overzealous audience member:)* I didn't laugh when I saw your mother. *(To class:)* She's a boricua, that's Puerto Rican. She runs the model laundromat for my father's Laundryland franchises.

Isn't she beautiful? Bet you'd like to get near her, huh? Not if she was your moms, you wouldn't. 'Cause if she was your moms she'd make you read the encyclopedia before you go to bed every night. And I have to finish volumes M to T before I get my Christmas present, which I don't even want 'cause I know it's going to be more encyclopedias. My mother says she's doing it because she loves me. Well, I don't know if love can kill, but it's getting real close.

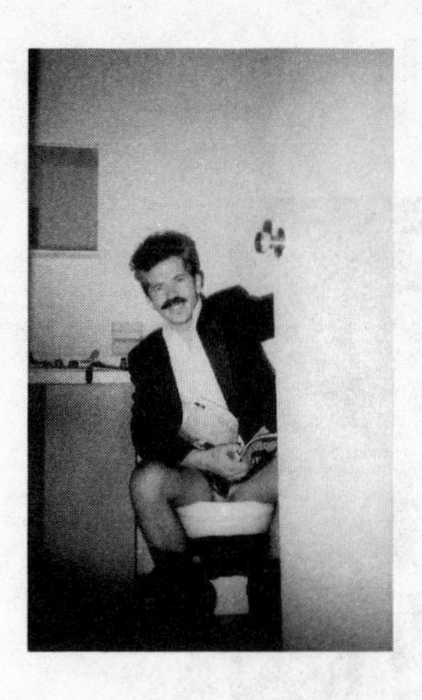

This is my father, Felix. He's Colombian. *(To classmate:)* What did you call my father? Mister Gabrielli, he called my father a drug dealer. *(To classmate:)* I'mma kick your ass. I'll take care of it, Mister Gabrielli. *(To audience member as if student in class:)* Did you ever kiss a rabbit between the ears? *(Pulls his pockets out.)* Go ahead. Kiss it. Kiss it. You asked for it, stupid. Stupid! *(Mumbles curses under breath and sucks teeth as he returns to center stage.)*

We have to live with my uncle and Aunt Ofelia so we can pay rent, 'cause my father takes all the money that should be ours and he gives it to his nasty girlfriends. Now can you guess which is his most favorite nasty girlfriend?

Is it Enigma?

Or Eutopia?

Or is it Yolanda?

I think it's the one with the guilty sweaty pits. *(Points to Yolanda's armpit.)* Aha!!

(Turns slide projector off.) I'm not supposed to tell you this, I'm not supposed to tell you this. You can't make me! You can't make me! All right, you win! I'm gonna tell you anyway. My mother was going through my father's pants and she found a letter from Yolanda. So she set all my father's pants on fire. *(Walks to stage left, set up as laundromat, and removes burned pair of shorts from one of the machines. Shows audience, then throws back into machine, slams door, and returns to center stage.)* And my father came home and caught her and called her "la negra india puta

inmunda del carajo"—"the nastiest black Indian ho of hell." And my mother cursed right back, "Tú eres un maricón, malparido y guevón." Look it up! And my father smacked my moms *(Mimes.),* so she ran and told my grandmother and my grandmother said, "Bueno, tú lo mereces"—"Good, you deserve it"—in her nasty parrot voice. And my mother gave her the evil "Chupame la teta!"—"Suck my titty!" And my grandmother reslapped my moms. *(Mimes all action.)* And my mom jumped on her and started choking her and then my father came into the room and grabbed my mom in a half-nelson and I jumped on him and started kickin' him and punchin' him and kickin' him *(Starts having an asthma attack.)* and he pushed me off and told me, "Go to your room and mind your business." So I went to my room. *(Walks to bedroom, stage right, and sits on foot of bed.)* 'Cause I got a headache, like when you drink milk too fast. And I knew they were going to kill themselves and I didn't want to hear it, so I just closed my eyes and put my fingers in my ears. *(Stands up, eyes closed, fingers in ears, and dances, singing:)*

Who's in the house?
Miggy's in the house.
"M" to the "I" . . . *(Changes tempo.)*
Nice and smooth and funky,
I'm a hip-hop junkie.
All I wanna do is hm hm to you
(Pelvic thrust.).

And when I pulled my fingers out of my ears and opened up my eyes, my father had moved out.

And I'mma miss him. Especially when he's drunk. 'Cause when he's drunk—oh, my God, he becomes the nicest man in the world. And he hugs me and kisses me and tells me that I'm his favorite son. And he begins to cry and cry and pulls out his maracas and tells how he almost played with Carlos Santana. Oh, my God, it's so much fun.

Then every holiday, I take all my savings and wait outside of Liquor World until I find somebody to buy me a big bottle of Colt 45 as a present for my father.

(Turns projector back on.) Okay, this the last shout out. This is the last skankless shout out and it goes to: my homes, my partner . . . Ivan!

(Chants:) Go chubby. Go chubby. Get stupid. Get stupid. Buggin' out y'all! Come on, stand up, Ivan, don't be shy. Me and Ivan are real close 'cause we came up with this game at the Fresh Air Fund camp this summer.

'Cause look how much fun we're having. So we came up with this game—spit basketball, where everyone had to spit in a bucket and the first person to get twenty-one won. And this big kid came along all uninvited and pushed Ivan, so I had to play him. And I beat him. And I don't know what came over him, 'cause all I said was, "I murdelized you. I destroyed you. Miggy's in the house!" And the sore loser picked up the bucket and poured it all over me and said, "Get out of my country, you stupid ugly spic!" Now I could of beat him up so bad, 'cause when you're angry, oh, my God, you can beat up people who are a million zillion trillion times your size.

But I didn't do nothing. 'Cause I didn't want to act like it counted. So I just stared at the kid and said, "Yes, yes, yes, I *am* a spic. I'm . . . I'm spic—tacular! I'm spic—torious! I'm indi—spic—able!"

And I stared at him and stared at him till he couldn't take it no more, and me and Ivan rode our bicycles off into the sunset.

Later on that night, in our tent, me and Ivan figured out that since we were spics, then our whole families must be spic-sapiens mondongo-morphs, and that when we have picnics together it's a spic-nic. And we made a promise to each other that no matter where we went or what we did, our whole lives would be nothing less than a Spic-O-Rama! *(Lights down.)*

KRAZY WILLIE

(When the lights come up, the headlights of the car pop on behind the chain-link fence and we hear banging coming from under the car. Krazy Willie slides from underneath the car on a dolly wearing his Desert Storm hat with the brim folded up off his face, dark Ray-Bans, a

football jersey lifted over his head and worn across his shoulders, camouflage pants, and combat boots with his BVDs sticking out. He sports a Vandyke goatee and holds a can of beer in a brown paper bag. He looks up to a window across the street, beyond the audience.)

KRAZY WILLIE: *(To his friend, Chewey, stage right:)* This is the shit! Chew, this is the shit! *(Jumps on hood of car; radio comes on.)* It's over for her, man, down by law. *(To window:)* Yo, yo, Yvonne. Krazy rules! Yo, Yvonne, I dedicate this song to you, baby. *(Kicks car, starting music.)* Krazy rules! Check this out.

(Sings to music:)

She was black as the night
Krazy was whiter than white

(To Chewey:) Yo, don't jump in, man, you throw me off. Shut the fuck up! *(Sings to Yvonne again:)*

Danger danger when you taste brown
sugar
Krazy fell in love overnight

Yo, yo, Yvonne. Yvonne, come on, baby! I'm giving you another chance. How about it, baby? *(Pauses.)* What do you mean, why do we both have to go? Because it's our fucking wedding, that's why!

Just shut up and listen! *(Sings:)*

Nothing bad it was good
Louie had the best that he could
When he took her home to meet his
momma and papa
Louie knew just where he stood

(Interrupted by voice from offstage hollering for him to shut up. Yells back:) Yo, am I singing to you? So mind your business! I'm singing to my alleged bride. I've got your off-key right here, motherfucker. *(Pauses.)* Go 'head, call the cops. You can kiss my culo! *(Moons figure offstage and sings:)*

Louie Louie Louie Louieee

(Screams to onlooker:) Take a good look, motherfucker. *(Sings:)*

Louie Louie Louie Louaaa . . .
She was black as the night . . .

(Pulls up pants, signals Chewey to cut radio, and yells up at window again:) Yvonne, do you see the things I'm doin' for you, baby? Goddammit, I know you hear me. I see your shadow—I know that big ole coochie anywhere. All right, Yvonne, you're leaving me no choice. *(Pulls gun from pocket.)* I'll do it. I'll do myself in. *(Puts gun in mouth.)* I'll blow out my brains. *(Puts gun in crotch.)* All right, Yvonne, I'm gonna shoot the thing you love most. *(Pauses.)* Damn, is nothing sacred to you?! *(Jumps off car.)*

I can't believe that fuckin' shit! Shut up, Chew. It ain't over till I say it's over. I'll house her. I'mma school her. *(Climbs over fence.)* Yo, Yvonne, if I can't have you nobody can. I ain't goin' out like that. *(Aside:)* She thinks she's all that. *(To window:)* Yvonne, you think you're Miss Subway 1992, don't you? *(Goes for pay phone. Mumbles under breath:)* Heads will roll, butts will be kicked, faces will be slapped, feelings are gonna be hurt.

(On the pay phone:) What do you mean I gotta put a quarter in? I'm only calling across the street. I went to Desert Storm—you should give it to me for nothing. . . . Bitch! Reach out and touch this . . . *(Steps back, shoots phone, then puts gun in crotch by mistake.)* Damn, that shit is hot! *(Pours beer down pants to put out sting.)* Damn, that shit is cold!

(To Chewey:) Do I deserve this? Do I deserve this? I'm a hero, man. Why is she dogging me like that? All I did was say, "Look, look, baby, I'm just back from the greatest victory America has ever had and I need some time to get my head together. So let's explore the world around us—see other people, but just to test the strength of our relation . . . cha cha-cha cha-cha cha-cha."

All right, busted. What I was really thinking is: Fuck, I can score any nena I want 'cause I'm young, gifted, and Latino. Word, let me tell you. Yo, I know I'm not no Arnold Schwartz-a-nigger. You know, that's a name that happens to offend black people twice, you fugly puta-head.

Well, she's on my jock, playing hurt. *(Imitates Yvonne:)* "All you wanna do is skeeze. That's all you wanna do. 'Cause ever since you came back you got no money. You never take me out. You never buy me pretty things. You're twenty-nine years old and nowhere, hanging out with losers." She was talking about you, Chew. Why can't she just lower her standards? I did. She's forever telling me how sorry she is that Andy Garcia is married—like she had a shot!

But I persist and get my wish. Pero, ojo what you wish for, Chewey, porqué you might get it!

So, I steps. I go to the beach to reconnoiter and—may I tell you, little brother man? It is like paradise. Every type of mad girl is there—las morenitas, las negritas, hasta las feitas. And I'm rappin' at this one and I'm rappin' at that one. And the next thing I know, the sun has set and I have rapped to every single one of them and got—nada. Culo. Dick. Just mine, that's it.

So I fall back to Yvonne's crib on the double and I weasel her. Oh, I'm seriously weaselin' her. "Yo, yo, yo, baby. It's a miracle! This one day has been enough for me. I've pulled myself together." And she's all, "What are you doing here? I thought we were supposed to be testing the strength of our relationship." *(Sucks teeth.)* "Huh?" *(Sucks teeth.)* "Mister War Hero. Hmm? Hmm? Hmm?" *(Sucks teeth again.)* If she would of sucked her teeth one more time, Chew . . .

So what do I do? I have to retrench and go to the usual—begging. "Take me back, baby! I was a bobo, tú sabes. War heroes say and do stupid things sometimes. I was just going through a lot of pressure"—always blame it on pressure, Chew. When in doubt, psychologize—"So I'm going through a lot of pressure, but I'm feeling a lot better now. So why don't you suck my dick?" Na, I didn't say that! But it's the thought that counts!

But then I bust out with, "Yo, baby, let's get married. 'Cause, I'm going to take care of you like no man has ever taken care of a female. And as a bonus—as a bonus—I'mma let you have my babies."

But I don't see her respondin', verdad? And I'm getting suspicious. 'Cause she's looking way too happy for her. So I kick it to her real dead dead calm and nonchalant, you know me. "Did you meet anyone or anything happen for you today . . . cha cha-cha cha-cha. And she kicks it back just as frosty, "Oh, no, why?" Qué mentirosa. Qué embustera. I know she's lying to me, man. 'Cause my mother said to me, "Yo, mijo, women will lie to you. I'm the only woman who will tell you the truth." So I but play her right back. "Come on, baby, I'm not gonna get mad. It was my idea, right? So did you get lucky and shit? 'Cause if we can't be honest and trust each other what have we had, baby?"

Boom, she fesses that she's already had one smokin' date today and she has another coming up in a half hour to take her to the Palladium on Tropical Night. "And thank you so much for suggesting this, 'cause I'm finding out so much about myself that I did not know before. And now could you please leave?" Yo, I stop hearing her talk and all I see is her mouth moving and getting bigger and bigger and bigger. *(Mimes with hand.)*

And she's buggin', "Get out of my house! I knew you were gonna go crazy, Krazy. You're just like your father." And I say, "Well, you're just like my mother." And she says, "You're hopeless!" And I say, and I say . . . What did I say? *(Pauses, then shouts.)* "Fuck you!" 'Cause I couldn't think of nothing better to say.

P.S., next thing I know I'm walking all the way from the fucking projects to Jackson fucking Heights. And I'm thinking three things: a) She used me, b) I helped her use me, and 3) I wish her father had used a condom.

(Chewey makes to leave.) Come on, man, where you going? What's up with that? Come on, don't be a pussy. Stick with me. Yo, you got no place to go, Chew. You a loser too, puta-head.

(To Yvonne:) Go ahead, ho. You know what I'm going to do? I'mma give you to five, then I'm gonna kill you, bitch. One Mississippi. Two Mississippi. *(Pulls out gun.)* No, no, you know what I'mma do? I'mma go to the Palladium and do a Happy Land Two. That's what I'm gonna do. *(Kicks and smashes his head against the fence.)*

(To Chewey:) Chewey man, help me out! It hurts like coño. I can't live without her. If I were to make love to another woman right now I'd still be making love to Yvonne. 'Cause she's the only woman that didn't make me feel like a zero. That's why. And how am I going to go to my wedding womanless? My father's gonna give me so much beef—oh, my God, you don't know!

God, I miss the seventies. It was the best time of my life: Huggy Bear, angel dust, the Partridge Family . . . *(Breaks into song:)*

I was sleeping,
And right in the middle of a good
  dream,
Like all at once I wake up
From something that keeps knocking at
  my brain.
Before I go insane
I hold the pillow to my head
(Mumbles next two phrases:)
I think I love you!
I think I love you!

What do you mean, get another woman? If I could get another woman do you think I'd be out here suffering like this?! If I got another woman you know what that would do to Yvonne? Another woman would make her loca. Another woman would make her homicidal. Another woman would make her . . . appreciate my finer qualities!

Oh, my God, Chew, I'm a genius! I'm a fucking genius. I found my salvation. I need to borrow your woman. *(Pauses.)* Why you comin' outcha face like that? I'd do it for you.

Come on, Chew, friends don't let friends stay dissed. And may I remind you, Mister Ungrateful Ingrate, the time I went down to the draft board as your little fuckin' boyfriend to get you out: "If you want a chick with a dick call nine-seven-oh Kathy." And *I'm* the one who ended up going to Desert Storm. I risked my life, shot people who look like us but with towels on their heads, to protect your American way of life. And then when I ask you for one little fucking favor—one little fucking favor—this is what I get? You un-American fuck! I can't even look you in your face. Asqueroso. Porquería. Inútil. *(Pauses.)* That's a lot better.

Okay, okay. Your mission, dog-face Chew, is to authorize your female, Epiphany, to marry me at seventeen hundred hours. Then we'll rendezvous at Our Lady of Suspicious Miracles as schedulized. 'Cause as soon as I peeps Yvonne bustin' in through the church doors, I'mma skip the "I do's"! I'm gonna ram my tongue so far down Epiphany's throat that when I pull back babas gonna be drippin' off her chin. *(Closes eyes, vividly mimes simultaneous tongue insert and pelvis grind.)* And I'm gonna press her so close she's gonna *know* I'm not circumcised.

And she won't be able to take it no more. Right. *(Pauses. To Chewey:)* No, *Yvonne* won't be able take it no more. Epiphany's gonna be having a great time. *(Back to fantasy:)* And she'll let out a scream. One of those you can hear in Jersey. "No, baby, no! I'm sorry, baby. I do, I do." And I'll say, "You do? You do? Well, baby, I . . . *don't*!" *(Pulls in fist in silent triumph.)* Ouch!!! Hurtin', hurtin'. Just like she hurt me, la majadera.

Then, finally, I'll put her out of her misery . and marry her. And I'll give Epiphany back you. Better than ever. And I'll be large. I'll the flavor with my cinnamon goddess back my arm where she belongs. *(Sings:)*

> Metale semilla a la maraca pa que
> suene
> cha cu cha cucu cha cu cha

You know what time it is? Synchronize.
Operation Recapture Yvonne is in full effect.
Attention! *(Pulls himself erect.)* Present arms!
(Swigs beer.) Forward . . . march! *(Sings:)*

> Your left, your left
> Your left, right, left.
> My back is aching, my
> belt's too tight,
> My cojónes are shaking
> from left to right.

Double time.

> Your left, your left,
> Your left, right, left.
> Frankenstein stole my wine
> That dirty motherfucker does it all the
> time. . . . *(Marches offstage. Lights down.)*

RAFAEL

(A spotlight beams on, illuminating Raffi, standing stage right in front of a triptych of mirrors. He wears a blond wig, blue contacts, and a robe that only exposes his legs and black-socked feet.)

RAFAEL: *(To mirror:)* If you pricketh *(Stabs air with saber.)* a Latino doth he not bleedeth? If you tickleth a Latino doth he not giggleth? *(Breaks into a falsetto giggle, as if being tickled.)*

(Lights up. To audience:) Do you like my British accent? Do you think it's real? I'm not telling you. Do you like my albino looks? Do you think they're real? I'm not telling you that either.

I *will* tell you that I'm on the verge of a major breakdown—breakthrough—breakthrough in my heretofore minor career.

You see, I am an understudy at the not-for-profit production of *The Canterbury Tales.* Yes, yes, someone finally took ill so I'm going on as the cuckolded innkeeper's manservant's best friend's friend's . . . friend. *(Spins around.)* Regarde . . . *(Recites with old English music playing:)*

> Whan that Aprill with his shoures sote,
> The droghte of Marche hath perced to the
>   rote,
> And bathed every veyne in swich licour
> Of which vertu engendred is the flour.

(Snaps fingers and music turns off.) You got it? It's a *major* opportunity. Any actor in his right mind would kill for it. Besides, acting jobs are like sex: all around, but I don't seem to be getting any. You know what I mean?

(Walks to far side of bed and removes robe, revealing a black-and-white vertically-striped button-down shirt and black-and-white polka-dot boxer shorts. Pulls on a pair of black supertight stretch jeans.) But I'm not taking any chances this time. Oh, no! I'm wearing height enhancement shoes, to get that *lengthy* look. *(Displays black Frankenstein platform shoes with white stripes on the sides of the platforms, then puts them on.)* And I'm also going to be wearing this vertically striped shirt to get that *lengthy* look. *(Displays shirt.)* And I'm also going to be stuffing my shorts *(Rapidly removes forty or fifty tissues from box one at a time while speaking.)* to get that . . . yes, that's right, that *lengthy* look. *(Stuffs huge wad of tissues into boxers, then buttons jeans around the bulge, which sticks out the open fly.)*

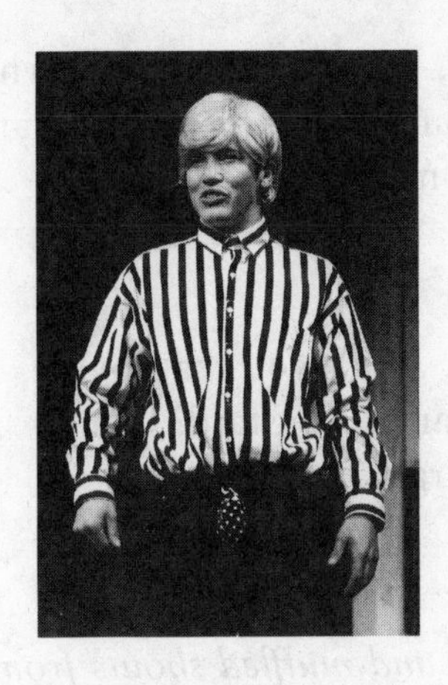

(*Gazes at reflection in the mirror, then down at his stuffed shorts. Recites with Scottish accent:)* "Is this a dagger which I see before me? The handle towards my . . . my . . . my . . . " *(To mirror:)* Excuse me, squire, are you that actor? Aren't you that famous actor? *(To audience:)* Guilty as charged.

(Feigns shame.) All right, I confess. You were going to find out anyway. . . . *(To audience:)* Please look me in the face! The rumors are true. I am the love child of Sir Laurence Olivier. Here's the true untold story. Laurence—Larry—met me mum in Puerto Rico while shooting *The Boys From Brazil.* Me mum was pressing his trousers . . . *(Mimes and sings:)* "I want to live in America—" when Larry sneaks up behind her in his undies

(Mimes.), grabs her bum, and whispers, "Ooh, I like young girls—their stories are shorter." Et voilà, mon frères! Je suis ici.

(To mirror:) Excuse me, aren't you that love child? Aren't you that famous bastard? *(To audience:)* Guilty as charged.

(Banging and muffled shouts from offstage. To bedroom door:) No, William, I'm not coming out. *(Pauses.)* I don't care! *(Pauses.)* No, I wouldn't attend your wedding if it was on *Star Search*. *(Pauses; rehearses sword fight.)* I don't have to come out and fight like a man. *(Elaborately flings cape over shoulders.)* I'm an actor, you gender-specific fascist. *(As he continues to talk, he puts a big jeweled cross on a gold chain around his neck. The look now resembles an Elizabethan costume.)* William, do you realize that you are a biological accident? Oh, yes, Mister Y-chromosome, why don't you go play with your little pre-woman? *(Imitating Willie badly:)* "Yo, Yvonne, let's get married, join the army, travel the world, meet interesting people and kill them." *(Aside:)* Yes, William, you're a hero . . . and so is a Blimpie.

(To audience:) I'm sorry. I'm very sorry. I must apologize for my brother. He's been on edge ever since Yvonne made a play for me. I'm not bragging, I'm sharing.

You see, I was working at Tele . . . Tele . . . How do you say it? Telemundo? I was dubbing movies at the time. You might remember me as the voice of Curly, in Spanish. *(Does impression of Curly:)* "Wooop. Pues claro. Un sinvergüenza, eh? Nyauh, nyauh! Pues yo debo."

Yvonne comes down to the studio to see what goes on behind the scenes. Well, no sooner are we alone than my slight hint of masculinity whips her into insensate desire, and being the occasional heterosexual that I am, I allowed her to have her way with me. But whilst our anatomies were coinciding, I could not stop thinking, "My life has no real purpose, no aim, no direction. I'm in complete self-denial, and yet I'm truly happy. I don't get it. What am I doing right?" And I looked down and I had lost the will. *(Addresses a male audience member:)* You know what I'm talking about? I knew you would. *(To all:)* So I faked an orgasm. I had never done this before in my life, but it's really quite simple: *(Mimes:)* I flipped her over on her front. I moaned and carried on—"Oh, oh"—pulled out, and spat on her back. I felt terrible. It was the first false note in an otherwise flawless performance.

(To mirror:) Are you that actor? Excuse me, squire, aren't you that famous actor? *(To audience:)* Guilty as charged!

Oh, God, I don't want to be with anyone whom I love more than myself. *(Inspects reflection.)* I'm not black. I'm not white. What am I? *(Sudden horror.)* I'm urine-colored, I'm actually urine-colored! *(Composes himself and adjusts wig. Shuts mirror triptych.)*

Well, I don't know why people insist on knowing themselves. It's hard enough to know what to wear. *(Crosses room to window.)* Oh, I don't care. I don't care. I'm not going to do anything I'm supposed to any more. I'm going home.

(Opens bedroom window and a Spanish Harlem–type cacophony invades room. Slams window shut. Silence.) It's so hard being Elizabethan in Jackson Heights. *(Walks toward television, next to mirror.)* But I don't care. I'm going to jet myself to London, nonetheless. I'll mingle with the palace pageantry. Have a fling with Di or Fergie. Perhaps Di *and* Fergie.

(A video of Laurence Olivier as the rabbi talking to Neil Diamond in The Jazz Singer *plays on a television above the mirror.)* Oh, look, it's me loving father, Laurence. *(To Laurence:)* Hello, Daddy. I'm coming to visit you.

LAURENCE: *(On screen.)* No!

RAFAEL: Yes, I'm going to live with you! *(Exits out the window.)*

LAURENCE: No!! I have no son!!!

RAFAEL: *(Peeks through window back at audience.)* You do now, ducky! *(Lights down.)*

JAVIER

(Stage dark. Dim spot follows Javier as he makes his way onstage in a wheelchair. His body is twisted beneath a very baggy gray sweat suit and white socks. He speaks slowly, with great effort, and occasionally drools.)

JAVIER: Okay, Miggy, turn the camera on. *(Brighter spot flicks on from wing. Sings:)*

For he's a jolly good fella,
For he's a jolly good fella...

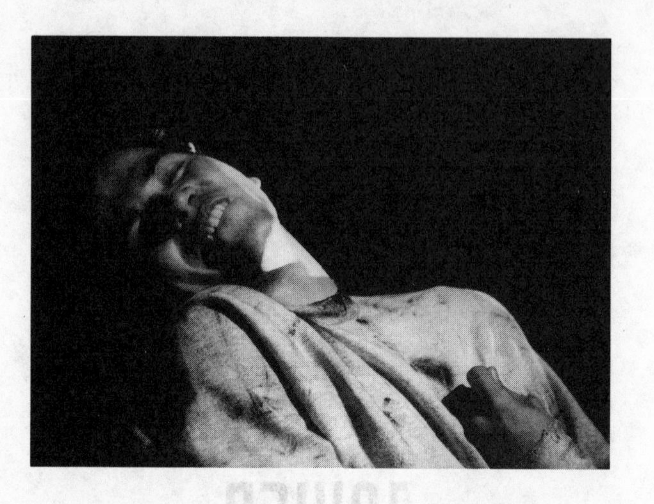

Willie, Willie . . . you're finally getting married. My condolences. You found a girl to stay with you. She must either be really ugly or really stupid. I wish you the best.

Mom, I'm sure you're looking as beautiful as ever. I'm sorry, I would of sent something sooner, but I probably spent it on a bottle or something. But, congratulations on the new little girl. Still overpopulating the planet, huh? We should just start that one-child policy the Chinese have; then we won't be starving to death, producing so much garbage.

Oh, yeah, pollution starts at home, Mom. Don't eat the tuna. The chicken's bad too, it's got salmonella. The beef has too much tetracycline. Vegetables have too many fucking pesticides. Can't drink the water—it has fluorocarbons. Can't breathe the air. Can't sit in the sun—no ozone. Can't sleep—noise pollution. TV rots our minds. . . . Well, I'm fine, and I hope you're all doing well.

Hope I'm not disturbing this little dinner party. Just turn me off anytime. Like you always do.

(Bitter laugh.) I know right about now Dad's saying to himself, "Enough of this shit. There's Yolanda. How can I get her in the bathroom and do her?" Well, fuck your sex life, Dad! This is my moment. And I wanna talk about my sex life. See, we're really not so different, you and me. We both have somewhat of a sexual problem. And the problem is that we both want to have sex. But only one of us can. Where's the justice in that? Oh, I've tried everything. I'm exhausted. I've explored all my fantasies and theirs. I've had women wear everything. I've tried every technique from the Kama-sutra to the Pink Pussy Cat.

I even went so far as to go to a sex therapist, but the access ramp only went to the second floor. So I got stuck with a dominatrix, Mistress Vanna Blanca, who stripped me naked, handcuffed me, wrestled me to the ground, then whipped my ass till it was raw.

She made me confess to things I never even knew existed. Ordered me to "suck and fuck and cook and clean. Now stop slobbering, you pig. And get on all fours and get banged like a bitch." And believe you me, Dad, I wanted to obey. But the only thing I wanna be good for I'm not even good at.

And this Vanna, well, I call her my girlfriend. She's the only one who ever loved me. And I can't please her, so I told her to get it wherever she can but not to fall in love. I don't know how long I can keep her like this. Tell me, Dad, how does it feel when you're inside them and you cum? Does the universe open up and for one moment you are made equal with the gods? You're a mambo king, an Aztec lord, an Inca prince. You're just every Hernandez and Fernandez! Isn't it wild, Dad? I'm telling you how it is!

You know, if this reincarnation thing is true, I'm definitely coming back as a blue whale. They're the largest species in the world. Can you imagine what an orgasm must be like for them? It must be huge.

If I could have an orgasm, then I could have a family, and if I could have a family I wouldn't fuck it up like you did. I know you're ashamed of me. But I'm more ashamed of you.

But don't worry about old Javier. I always get along without you somehow. I dance in my thoughts. I play basketball in my mind. And I get off in my dreams. See, Dad, everybody gets their *(Winces with headache pain.)* discount dream.

Do you ever think of all the people who have died? How many souls are out there trying to get into our bodies? Even mine. I think that's where we get headaches from. And I'm getting a headache right now, so I gotta go. Felicitaciónes, Willie, maybe I'll be there for Christmas. I don't know. Probably not.

(Shifts to leave, then thinks of one more thing.) Dad, remember that night when this gang was making fun of me outside the house: "Mira el mutant, mira el mutant." And you came out and you screamed, "What the hell are you doing to my son?" And you grabbed this guy's shirt so close he could taste your spit and you told him if you ever saw them on the block again you were going to kill each and every one of them. . . .

I fell in love with you that night, Dad. I couldn't believe you were the same man I had hated for all those years. Why can't you be that dad now?

Turn it off, Miggy! Vanna, get 'im out of here. *(Lights down.)*

GLADYZ

(Lights up. A funky seventies song plays. Gladyz is doing aerobics by the dryers while smoking a cigarette. She has a long, curly, hennaed mane of hair held back by a fuchsia headband, heavily mascaraed eyes, and bright red lips. She wears a fuchsia spandex off-the-shoulder top, fake Pucci spandex tights, a fantasy-gold necklace, big hoop earrings, a little gold watch, and spiked white pumps. In

front of the row of dryers is a bench with a baby carriage nearby and a can of Diet Coke on the ground.)

GLADYZ: Work it . . . and work it . . . and work it . . . *(To Miggy, stage left:)* Go on, Miguelito, and play like a little gentleman. Mommy'll be right here doing her aerobics.

Miguelito, I said play nice. Don't rub soap in little Malaria's hair. Be a gentleman. And if you start to wheeze—sit down! No, not in the laundry basket, condenado. And use that inhaler, 'cause I don't want to spend my whole weekend in the hospital. What with Willie's wedding and all, I don't have the time, please.

(To Ofelia, downstage left:) I can't do this no more. No joda. All this just to be loved from the neck up.

(Picks handful of dirty laundry out of basket and inspects. To Miggy:) Miguelito, are these your brushstrokes? Mira, Ofelia, they're color-coded. Yellow in the front, brown for the back. *(Tosses clothes into machine, slams door.)*

(Coos to the baby in the carriage.) Ay, chichichita. Tan bonita la niña. Tan preciosa. *(To Ofelia:)* Ay, tenía que ser mia. *(To baby:)* Anisette. Tan cute. Anisette.

(Waves to Esperanza, downstage center:) Hola, nena! Esperanza—bring your child-bearing hips over here. How you doing? Niña, you look terrific. Let me tell you, twenty children haven't slowed you down one bit. *(Pauses.)* I'm just teasing you. You look good. You don't look chubby at all. You on a diet? I'm on a diet too, but what you see is a very tall woman trapped in a very short body.

Ay, Espy, you shouldn't have. *(Takes package from Esperanza. Shouts:)* Miguelito, Esperanza brought you some candy. *(Drinks from her Coke can and addresses Esperanza:)* You shouldn't. *(To Miggy:)* Say thank you. Always say thank you and please; that way you get more.

(To Esperanza:) Ay, mija, I can't stay and talk too long 'cause I'm going to lose my Krazy in a couple of hours. Sí, es sad, verdad. El primero, tú sabes. *(Whispers:)* It's not bad enough that that bruja Yolanda bed my Felix. But now her Cubanoid little heifer of a daughter is stealing my Willie.

(Back to Miggy:) Miguelito, don't interrupt me. Don't you see I'm talking? Don't come to me with your problems. You don't see me running to you every time I have a problem,

do you? *(Pauses.)* Ay, Dios mío. Don't get loud with me. If she takes your bicycle just push her off!

(To girlfriends:) Ooops. I hope our most sacred lady of the hussies didn't hear me.

(Gladyz sees Miggy knock Malaria down.) Oopsie! *(Shouts:)* I'm sorry, Yolanda. I hope Malaria's okay. Miguelito, come over here right now! No joda zángano, lo cojo y lo vuelvo mierda. Le hago que le salgan plátanos por el culo. Come over here right now! I should slap you silly, cabróncito. *(Whispers confidentially to Miggy:)* I'm glad you knocked her down—just don't get caught next time. Go back and play like a little gentleman.

(Shouts:) I scolded him for you, Yolanda, now he's crying. I hope you're happy?

(To Esperanza:) Ay, mija, what did you do to your hair? What did you do to your hair? That is a do and a don't together. *(Snaps her fingers. Pauses.)* We marry beneath us—all redheads do. *(Pauses.)* No, this is not a hair weave. This is hair fusion. *(Puts cigarette on baby carriage.)* I could do that and more to my hair and Felix would not even notice. The romance has gone poof . . . limp. Tú sabes, like dead champagne. Ay, men today. *(Sighs.)* Ay. Ay. Ay. *(Baby coughs.)* Ay—Anisette! *(To Esperanza:)* She's trying to smoke. *(To baby:)* Ay, tan cute. Anisette, stop it. *(Pulls cigarette out of carriage and takes a big drag.)*

(To girlfriends:) Ay—look over there at that gorgeous papi! No, don't look. Now—look! No, don't look. Now. Isn't he gorgeous? He comes and does his jeans every day. The same jeans.

Ay, qué precioso. Isn't he ouch-looking? How do I look, nenas? Do I look okay? *(Pauses.)* Well, do I at least look good for me?

(She stands and strikes a seductive pose, then beckons to man.) Psst! Ksss. Ishmael. Ishmaelito. Yoo-hoo! *(To the girls:)* Isn't he ouch-looking? No invente papito. Me tiene—uutthh. *(Bites her hand.)* Ishmael . . . Ishmaelito . . . Ishy . . .

(To girlfriends:) Why is he talking to that buttless, anorexic third world desgraciada!

I can't believe it. That witch musta put a spell on him. Well, lookaher, do you see the way she dresses? Do you see the way she moves? It's obscene. It's disgusting. It's perverse. Oh, God, I wish I were her!

(Sniffs the air.) Ay fo, qué's eso? Is that you? What's that smell? Somebody's insides are rotten. Ay, please—it's the baby. Anisette. No joda. Somebody please change her for me! *(Pushes carriage away. It rolls down the aisle of machines toward backstage.)* Ay, Dios mío, it never stops. All this responsibility. All day it's clean this, wipe that, take care of this. No wonder animals eat their young. You know, it's only a matter of time before she'll turn on me. Mija, let me tell you—it's a mother's curse. You hate your mother until you become one and then you are filled with the deepest respect. *(Sighs and throws down cigarette butt.)*

I never had a chance to be independent. All
my life, somebody's always been on my tit.
That's why they're hanging so low. 'Cause
people don't like their women strong.
Especially Spanish women—forget about it!
We're just ornaments . . . female eunuchs.
We're just allowed to nurture and understand,
but God forbid we should go for what we
want, 'cause then you're a bitch.

Ofelia, you're lucky you can't have children. 'Cause you're free to do . . . to do . . . What is it that you do? Well, whatever it is that you do. Ever since I was seventeen I've been raising four—five—five children. *(Retrieves baby carriage.)* You know what that's like? One of these afternoons . . .

(Spies Miggy climbing on machines.)
Miguelito, if you fall off of that dryer and break your legs, don't come running to me.

(Takes a piece of chocolate cake from carriage. Eats while she speaks.) I wish I could change my name to Christmas or Electricity. Gladyz is so plain. Then everybody'd find me mysterious and I'd get invited to all the parties. I always wanted to have a life, one that I could talk about. 'Cause I had the brains but not the clothes—that's why I dropped out of high school.

Nenas, you know what I would like to do? You know what I'd like to do? I'd like to drink a pitcher of Yago Sant'Gria, rip off all my clothes, and run naked in the streets and hug all the ugly women and tell them that it's okay. There, I said it! I said it!

(To baby, who is fussing.) Ay. Qué te pasa, nenita? Chichichita, Anisette. She's having a bad dream. Shhh. Sana que sana, culito de rana. *(Pours Diet Coke into baby bottle. To Ofelia:)* Don't worry, it's diet. Suck it up. There you go. Qué linda. Tan cute.

You know, if I do only one thing right it's to make sure her life is nothing like mine. *(Lights another cigarette.)* Did I tell you? I had a bad dream last night myself. I dreamt my mother had died. And I woke up sweating and crying, tú sabes. And I went running into her room and I hugged and kissed her and told her how I loved her. And she slapped me right in the face—for waking her up. It's the story of my life. She never forgave me for putting her in a home, and I'll never forgive myself for taking her out.

All day long it's "Ay, mija, I'm gonna die. Ay, mija, I'm gonna die." I'm starting to like the sound of it. Oh, I know I'm the dark meat in my family. . . . And speaking of dark meat. *(Extracts a chicken leg from carriage and munches delicately. Smokes, munches, smokes, munches.)* Smoked chicken. Did you hear

about her buttlessness and somebody's husband? Aha, aha, mmmmm. May God strike me down. Que Dios me haga más vieja antes de mi tiempo if I'm lying to you. Yes, I heard it from a very reliable source. Someone said to someone who then told somebody else, then that somebody told me quite by accident, so I know it's true. No, not Rosi's. No, not Mirtha's. *(Tosses chicken leg into carriage.)* Did I say Agnes? *(Pauses.)* Yesss, it was Cookie. It was Cookie. Imaginate! And they're supposed to be best friends. See, mija, you can't trust other women, 'cause they'll say one thing to your front and another to your behind.

Mira, Esperanza, if I was two-faced do you think I'd be wearing this one? Por favor. Dios mío.

I'm not imagining things, Ofelia. She's trying to steal my Felix. Once upon a lie he vowed to be my one and only, but now . . . *(To customer:)* Excuse me, I'm talking! I'm sorry, Miss Lady, you can't get your money back. You take your chances in this laundromat. Jodona pendeja.

(Back to Esperanza:) Oh, he's out there wenching, mujeriando. One day they'll find I killed my husband and I'm gonna plead voluntary insanity.

(To another customer:) I'm sorry, Mister Man, I'm sorry. You got the Vegas machine—you gotta keep putting quarters in till one of them hits.

(To the ladies:) I'm thinking of letting Felix come back to the house. *(Pauses.)* Yes, but on probation. 'Cause as bad as he is, he's one of the better ones. It's a recession everywhere. Anyway, she's only this year's model. And if I catch him again—that's it. I'm taking the house and my boys and I'm going to make them the best little men of Jackson Heights.

(Sees Miggy pummeling another child.) Miguelito, papá, don't hit anybody unless they are down.

Ay, coño bendito, I didn't realize what time it was. I have to take the F train to el culo de New York. Miguelito, let's go.

(To the girls, as she collects her belongings:) Well, it's been muy fun. Bien nice y chévere. Chaito. Ofelia, could you close for me? And don't give any money back—it's the American way.

(Calls to Miggy:) Miguelito, come on, we're going to be late for the wedding. *(Pauses.)* Well, push her off if it's your bike. What are you, a boy or girl? Knock her down. That's it. See you, nenas. So long, Yolanda. See you at the wedding. If you can scrape yourself off the floor, you nasty bitch!!!! *(Pushes carriage off-stage. Lights down.)*

FELIX

FELIX: *(Offstage to Yolanda:)* That's very Spanish of you. It's gonna take more than a little spritz to put out my fire, baby.

(Felix walks onto center stage, where there is a spotlight. He is a middle-aged, corpulent man with graying hair and a thick black mustache. He wears a black tuxedo with a white

carnation on the lapel and black patent leather shoes. He is holding a mike in one hand and a glass of champagne in the other. Visibly drunk, damp, and disheveled, he mops his face with a handkerchief.) Epa! Epa! Qué rico! Sabrosito! Menealo!

Well, here we are at Grand Prospect Hall, where all your dreams come true. It's not the Magic Kingdom, but if you close your eyes, it's only a hop and a skip. We gotta push things along, 'cause the Herkowitz funeral is next. Grandma, you can stay.

Okay, I'm gonna sing a song. *(To band:)* Okay, knock it off. Let's give it up for the band. *(Applauds.)* You boys played real good. Thanks, boys. I'm gonna give you a big tip: Don't fry bacon in the nude. *(Drum and cymbal—ba dump ba.)* I'm gonna sing a song, 'cause my father sang at my wedding. And I've selected a special tune for this occasion. 'Cause everybody thinks Colombians are in the Mafia, so we might as well take advantage of it. It goes something like this: *(Sings:)*

Speak softly love and hold me warm
against your heart
The trembling vows we made will live
until we die
I told the truth
Then lied some more
Porqué tú me haz jodido y no puedo
más
Y no es mi culpa
I said mm-hmm
She probably said mm-hmm
(Hums a line, then whistles.)

It's too painful. It brings back too many memories of my father and of Gladyz when she was young and beautiful.

Ah, life! Tell me, isn't it moments like this that make you think about the meaning of life? I've been thinking a lot about it lately. Even the great philosophers have wrestled with this one and come up empty. What is life? Anybody! *(Sighs.)* What the fuck difference does it make? The first half is ruined by your parents and the second half destroyed by your kids. That's life!

Now, I know the newlyweds would be disappointed if I did not speak at length about matrimonio. So listen up, amigos y socios, Yvonne. Willie, as I told you from the time you were yo high, and I can never tell you enough: Lies, distortions, half-truths, and critical omissions are the glue to all relationships.

Uncle Brother, stop drinking like it's the end of the world. *(Pauses.)* No, it's not the blood of Christ. It's sangría. *(Pauses.)* Oh, go ahead and put a curse on me. I already live in New York—what more can you do to me.

(To newlyweds:) So I'm going to teach you two how to keep that matrimonio fresh and alive, when what you really wanna do sometimes is put a bullet through your head. Fantasize. Fantasize. There is absolutely nothing wrong with taking the body of a woman you desire and superimposing it over the tired old thing at home.

What else? What else? You're also gonna fight a lot, which is really a lucky thing 'cause sex is never as good as after a vicious fight . . . right, Gladyz? My little gladiatress. Nothing like rough sex! *(Barks.)*

When I was younger I used to have . . . what do they call that now? Anybody! Performance anxiety. Now I just look forward to giving it my best shot and coming out of it alive. Many a night I have come home to Gladyz and asked her for a little cabeza and she says, "I'm too tired, I'm too tired." And I tell her, "Baby, it'll be over before you know it. You won't feel a thing."

If I was a young puppy again, instead of the old dog that I am! Yvonne, yum, Yvonne, you look nice. There're so many things I could've done to your Bosco candy-coated thighs.

(To Willie who has shouted at Felix:) Hey, Willie, what are you getting so upset about? Oh, all of a sudden you're man enough to take me on? *(Takes off jacket.)* I never raised my hand to my father, 'cause if I had *(Begins sparring.)*, I wouldn't be here to punch you into place. Et tu, Raffi? Et tu? Go ahead, both of youse. You get the first punch, then I get a shot.

Back off, Gladyz, back off! What are you taking their side for? It's my money that paid for this hall. It's my hall, it's my liquor, it's my cake, and I'll do whatever the fuck I please. You wanna hit me too? *(Rolls up sleeves.)* So everybody here wants to take a shot at me. Come on, I'll take everybody on. Everybody except you, Ofelia. I never fight with ugly people . . . they got nothing to lose.

I'm not drunk. Never been more sober in my life. *(Pauses.)* No, baby, I've had to eat it for so long I've had it up to here. What this family needs es una enema grandisima! *(Nasty gesture.)*

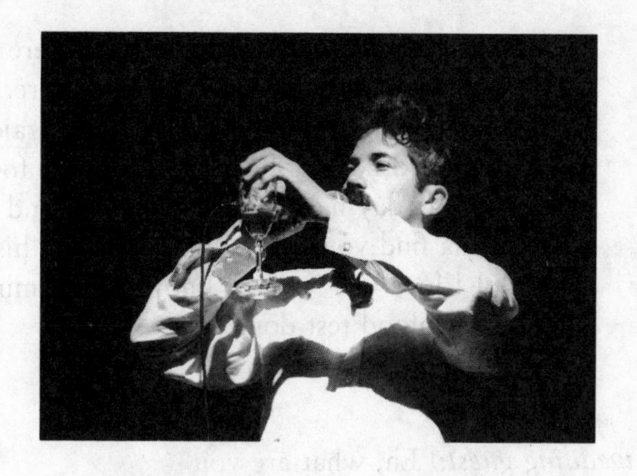

Shut up, I'm getting to the toast. Here's to Krazy Willie. What kind of name is that for a grown man, huh? To my firstborn. I love you, but you're a disappointment. I'm sorry, but you're a big disappointment. I couldn't make you a man. The war couldn't make you a man. What makes you think in your wildest dreams that this poor sixteen-year-old titty-bopper's got a shot? Don't run away from me. Everybody, look at the pussy go. *(To Yvonne:)* Don't worry, sweetheart, he always comes crawling back.

And here's to Raffi: to my son, who is an extra in his own family. I love you . . . in my own way. But you're a liar. You're a goddamn liar. Why do you refuse to acknowledge me as your father? Answer me! Answer me! Did I beat you? Did I abuse you? Maybe, maybe— but you have to be resilient in life.

Where's my favorite little nerd? Where is he? Miguelito, come over here. Come here, papá. Come over here. What are you so afraid of? Go ahead, keep following in Willie's footsteps and one day he's gonna stop short and you're gonna find your head going right up his ass. But I love you 'cause I know you're mine. I had a blood test done.

(To a wedding guest:) Eh, what are you whispering over there? Why don't you say it to my face? Let me tell you something. There's nothing Felix Leopardo Gigante hasn't heard already. A toast to myself: What can be said about me? That I tried to be more and better. That I tried not to make the same stupid mistakes my father made.

At least I was there for youse. I gave up a lot to provide for youse. I never told you this but I had a shot to travel with Carlos Santana. That's right—Mister Oye Cómo Va. He came up to me personally and said that I was the best maracas player he'd ever heard. Then Gladyz got pregnant with Willie, then wichoo, Raffi, and then Javier . . . *(Lowers head, overtaken by emotion.)* Oh, my God, Javier. And it destroyed my chance. 'Cause I could of played with one of the great Latin rock and rollers. Grabbed God by the ears and kissed him right smack on the lips. But I chose to stick it out and give you what I could, and what do I got? My memories. Youse . . . *(Pauses and reflects a moment.)*

I have a confession to make. Unbeknownst to Gladyz here, I had an affair once. I'm sorry, baby. I admit it. But it kept me from running away and it helped me to understand you. *(Pats gut.)* Kept me young. It's not that we men want more sex than women, it's that we want a different kind of sex. More often. Right, fellas? *(Silence.)* Well, don't all back me up at once. *(To Gladyz:)* Ever since you had the kids, you only want it when Jupiter aligns with Mars.

I ask myself, where would I be without you by my side? Pushing me, kicking me, nailing me to the wall. 'Cause deep in my heart, I believe that any woman can make love to a handsome man, but it takes a great woman to keep making love to an ugly pig like me. To my gordita.

Go, get out of here, go to him, Yvonne. You have my blessing. Enjoy your honeymoon. Why he's taking you back to the gulf, I don't know. But promise me, Yvonne, my new daughter, that you'll always be there to fix it, mend it, make it better, and if it doesn't work out then, remember, you always have family. And tell my son that no matter how much he hates me, I'll always be here for him, 'cause we're stuck with each other.

Now I want the rest of you to hurry up and enjoy the festivities. I gotta take a leak. *(Picks up jacket, trails offstage as lights go down.)*

Epilogue:

MIGGY

(Lights up. Miggy comes into his bedroom, dragging his feet. He is ready for bed, wearing his stocking cap, teeth with overbite, thick glasses, oversized blue-and-white flannel pajamas, and two different-colored tube socks dangling from his feet. He speaks in a low, sad voice.)

MIGGY: I lost my hero, Krazy. I lost my hero, Krazy. *(Mopes, then suddenly cheers.)* But I got all his stuff! *(Goes to his box.)*

(Playacts. As emcee:) Miggy, welcome to "Yo MTV Raps." We hear you're a great dancer.

(As himself:) Well, you can't believe everything you hears.

(As emcee, fake humble:) You've been selected out of millions of kids for this dance competition.

(As wildly enthusiastic self:) Okay, I'm a Sagittarius. I love chocolate ice cream.

(As emcee:) Go! *(Hits music.)*

(Dances, as himself.) Did I win yet? Did I win yet? I won! I won! What do I win?

(As emcee:) You win your own Nintendo Super Mario Brothers and a lifetime pass to Club MTV.

(As himself:) I won! I won! I'd like to thank all the little people who I had to step on to make it here. *(Gasping and wheezing, fishes inhaler from breast pocket and inhales a squirt.)*

(Anxious pause. To mother behind bedroom door.) Noise? What noise? I'm not doin' nothing. I'm just resting. *(Pauses.)* Yes, yes, yes. I'm already studying that old ridiculous encyclopedia—so there! You tell me things a million trillion zillion times that I forget 'cause you tell me so many times. *(Pauses.)* Na-ha. I'm not gonna go to sleep, 'cause that stupid old wedding took up my valuable time. *(Throws tantrum.)* Now I know why people get married. It's so they can have children and make somebody else's life miserable.

(Jumps from bed to chin-up bar and hangs.) I want to be a basketball player. I want to be a basketball player. God, please don't make me a jockey. Am I Michael Jordan yet?

No *(Lets go of bar, falls to bed)*, because my parents made me genetically deficient in height chromosomes. They must be punished.

(Leaps off of bed and establishes a mock court at the foot. As himself:) I herebywith take Mister and Missus Gigante to court.

(As counselor:) Your Honor, my client has suffered because of abuse and negligence.

(As himself:) Yes. I can't even take care of myself, so why do I have to take care of my useless sister and vacuum the dog? I'm a child, not a slave. And I don't want to go to the Fresh Air Fund with some family I don't even know, like a hostage. They could be murderers and have bones and skulls of other Fresh Air Fund victims in the refrigerator. *(Screams.)*

(As parents:) But Your Honor, we have done all we can. He just doesn't deserve anything. He won't finish his encyclopedias. He doesn't eat his vegetable goo. . . .

(As himself:) Objection, time out, illegal!

(As parents:) But Your Honor, we're doing everything—

(As judge:) Shut up!

(As parents:) But why?

(As judge:) Because it's the law. Go on, my son.

(As himself:) Thank you, Your Honor. They argue in Spanish so we won't understand what they are saying. But we speak Spanish too!

(As judge, to Miggy:) I herebywith give you custody of yourself to yourself.

(To parents:) And you must wear your dirty underwears on your heads. Recess.

(As himself, to mother behind bedroom door again:) I can't hear you, Mom. I'm a giant Ninja Turtle taco. *(Crawls under quilt that has Mutant Ninja Turtles all over it.)* Na-ah. I'm not gonna take that nasty medicine. Why don't you take it? *(Pauses.)* I didn't say nothing. I said thank you for reminding me, Mommy dearest. *(Pauses.)* Okay, don't take me to the hospital. I'm gonna report you to the ASPCA for child abuse.

(Hanging upside down over the edge of the bed. His head touches the ground. Muses to himself:) What if I killed myself? Then they'd be sorry. Here lies the most good boy Miggy who never got what he deserved. I'll say *yes* to drugs. *(Flings off quilt and shouts:)* Yes. Yes. Yes. Yes. Yesss!!

(To door:) Okay, shut up. I'm already goin' to sleep. *(To himself:)* God, I hate this house. I hate this family. I hate this asthma. I wish I were dead. I don't mean that, God. It's just for them. Okay?

(To door:) Mom? Mom? You know, Mom, it won't be long before I'm all grown up and one day you're gonna wake up and ask yourself, "Where did all the time go? Miggy is so big and I never let him have any fun. That must be why he never visits me anymore." And you'll have nasty elephant ankles and you'll drool and be deaf and lonely in a home. And they won't let you play either.

(Sound of parents fighting offstage filters through the door.)

(Sings with eyes closed and fingers in ears:)

Miggy's in the house, y'all
I said 'M' to the 'I' to the 'G' to the 'G'
to the
'Y,' y'all
I'm a hip-hop junkie . . .

I know what I'll do! I'll make my molecules vibrate so fast I'll be invisible and I'll run away, travel the world from galaxy to galaxy at warp speed, and . . . *(Jumps and grabs chin-up bar. Looks upward.)* God, if you make them stop, I'll be the best little boy in the whole world. *(Muffled shouts continue.)* Okay, God, I'm warning you! If you don't make them stop, I'm never gonna believe in you. Okay, you asked for it, I'mma take the Virgin Mary and tie her up, put her in a brown paper bag, and if you ever wanna see your mother again, you'll do what I tell you.

(Bar retracts, lifting Miggy heavenward.) I didn't say nothing, mean-head. *(Lights down.)*

ABOUT THE AUTHOR

JOHN LEGUIZAMO, as writer and performer, received critical acclaim and won the 1991 Obie and Outer Critics Circle awards for his first one-man show, *Mambo Mouth*. He obtained the 1992 Lucille Lortel Award for Best Actor in an Off-Broadway Play for his second, *Spic-O-Rama,* which won the Dramatists Guild's Hull-Warriner Award for Best Play of 1992. Both have been broadcast on HBO and the film version of *Mambo Mouth* received four ACE nominations.

Raised in Jackson Heights, Queens, Leguizamo studied drama at New York University, where he appeared in the award-winning student film *Five Out of Six*. He made his television debut as Calderon Jr. in *Miami Vice* and went on to appear in the films *Casualties of War, Revenge, Hangin' with the Homeboys,* and *Whispers in the Dark*. He co-stars in *Super Mario Brothers* with Bob Hoskins and Dennis Hopper, in *Carlito's Way* with Al Pacino and Sean Penn, and in the forthcoming buddy film *Nothing to Lose*. He is currently writing his first screenplay, *White Chocolate,* with Peter Askin, as well as a television comedy special, *House of Buggin'*.

Also available from Bantam Books
John Leguizamo's
MAMBO MOUTH
A Savage Comedy

Winner of Obie, Outer Critics Circle, and Vanguardia awards, John Leguizamo's *Mambo Mouth* is a riotous—and scathingly honest—look at Latino manhood. From Agamemnon, cable TV's Latin Lothario, to Loco Louie, the boom-box-bearing Puerto Rican kid, to Manny the Fanny, a transvestite prostitute whose weapons of choice are Krazy Glue and a king-size kitchen knife, here are seven unforgettable portraits that reveal the comically confused and frequently anguished individual behind the stereotypic mask of Hispanic machismo.

"Kaleidoscopic, hilarious and politically very incorrect."
—*Time*

"Brutally funny."
—*The New York Times*

"Bristles with the energy of secrets unleashed . . . Satire that is supple as well as raw."
—*The Village Voice*

Agamemnon

Live, baby, I'm always live. *(Show's mambo theme music begins. Agamemnon signals audience to clap.)* Work with me, people. Hola! Epa! Stop it, you're spoiling me. Hola, hola, people, and welcome to *Naked Personalities*, the most dangerous show on public access TV. Where we take an uncensored look at your most favorite celebrity—me! That's right. And for the few of you who don't know me *(winks)*, my name is Agamemnon Jesús Roberto Rafael Rodrigo Papo Pablo Pacheco Pachuco del Valle del Río del Monte del Coño de su madre *(pauses to swig from wine cooler and signals to cut music)* López Sánchez Rodríguez Martinez Morales Mendoza y Mendoza.

But you can call me handsome. Why not? I deserve it. *(Searches audience.)* You women are probably asking yourselves, is he or isn't he? Well yes, ladies, I am . . . married. But don't lose hope because my lawyers are working on it, and pretty soon I'm going to be out and about. So beware . . . grrrrrrrr! *(Rolls r's.)* But remember, ladies, I'm not omnipresent—only omnipotent. Huh! *(Pelvic thrust.)*

Loco Louie

(To Chonchi:) So where was I? Oh yeah—so check this out. I'm hanging by my lonesome, playing some hoops and shit, right? When Ninja comes along, and he's got this big box of caffeine pills that he got on a five-finger discount. And he tells me that it gives you the strength of ten men—if you know my meaning? You know my meaning! So I pop fifteen of those suckers right away, right? And I never even had coffee and shit.

So we're waiting for the shit to kick in, right? *(Whistles.)* And then one, two three—*(Goes rigid.)* We are human hard-ons. We are horny as shit, boy. All we can think about is fucking. All we can talk about is fucking. We are fucked. So we say, "Fuck it, let's go fuck!"

So what do we do? We jets over to Nilda's Bodega and Bordello. We had to, 'cause all this has been buildin' inside us since we were born, and we can't get any to save our lives—and it hurts. Uh-unh, it ain't for lack of trying. You know me, Chonchi—I don't limit myself to things that breathe. Word! *(Bugs.)*

Angel Garcia

(Pleadingly working the cop.) Desicoroonie, let me go, man! I swear I didn't do nothing. You're trying to incarcetize me for something I didn't do. I just had an argument with my woman, that's all. C'mon, you never disciplinify your women? I know you guidos, man. You're hot-headed just like we are.

(Confidential.) Check this out, Desico. Hear me out. I come home early, right? Boom. It's our anniversary, and I got some flowers, right? Boom. And I hear these suspicious noises, right? I know what's going on, but I can't believe she's that stupid to play me like that. Boom. I open up the bathroom door, and she's got my homeboy on top of her. Boom, boom, boom! You see what I'm saying?

That's right, a special romantic other. What am I supposed to do—sit there and ref? That's my woman, man! I love her so much, I'm gonna kick her ass. *(Punches wall. Then, under his breath:)* I'm not gonna let it get to me. Nothing's gonna get to me.

Pepe

Come on, ése. It's not like I'm stealing or living off of you good people's taxes. I'm doing the shit jobs that Americans don't want. *(Anger builds again.)* Tell me, who the hell wants to work for two twenty-five an hour picking toxic pesticide-coated grapes? I'll give you a tip: Don't eat them.

Orale, you Americans act like you own this place, but we were here first. That's right, the Spaniards were here first. Ponce de León, Cortés, Vásquez, Cabeza de Vaca. If it's not true, then how come your country has all our names? Florida, California, Nevada, Arizona, Las Vegas, Los Angeles, San Bernardino, San Antonio, Santa Fe, Nueva York!

Tell you what I'm going to do. I'll let you stay if you let me go.

Inca Prince

We come from so many famous people, Carlitos. People who have done this and done that. . . . Like who? Like who. Like Maria Consuelo Cleopatra. . . . What, you didn't know she was Latina? Sure—as a matter of fact, Marc Antonio Rodríguez was madly in love with her.

And how about Guilliam Shakesperez? Yeah, Guilliam Shakesperez. He wrote some great stuff—*Romero y Julieta, Macho Do About Nothing, The Merchant of Venice-Zuela.* "Alas, alack, alook and a lick, hither, thither, fie, fie, fie. . . ." You didn't know he was a quarter Latino? Oh, yeah. As a matter a fact, inside of every great person there's always a little Latino.

Crossover King

Konichi-wa. Dozo ohairi kudusai. Hai! *(Jerks head.)* Welcome and welcome, Latino-sans, to the Crossover Seminar. Now, this could very well be the biggest investment of your entire life, so please hold your questions until the end. Hai! *(Jerks head, then sips water.)*

You too could be a crossover success. It's up to you *(points to an audience member)* and you *(points to another)*. This is purely a scientific method. There are no placebos or messy ointments.

Now, what exactly is a crossing over, you ask? That's a good question. Crossing over is the art of passing for someone that you are not in order to get something that you have not. Because there is no room in the corporate upscale world for flamboyant, fun-loving spicy people. So get used to it. I did.